DINNER IN AN INSTANT

DINNER IN AN INSTANT

75 MODERN RECIPES
FOR YOUR
PRESSURE COOKER,
MULTICOOKER,
+ INSTANT POT®

MELISSA CLARK

CLARKSON POTTER/PUBLISHERS
NEW YORK

Copyright © 2017 by Melissa Clark
Photographs copyright © 2017 by Christopher Testani

Published in the United States by Clarkson Potter/Publishers,
an imprint of the Crown Publishing Group, a division of
Penguin Random House LLC, New York.
crownpublishing.com
clarksonpotter.com

CLARKSON POTTER is a trademark and POTTER with colophon
is a registered trademark of Penguin Random House LLC.

Library of Congress Cataloging-in-Publication Data
Names: Clark, Melissa, author.
Title: Dinner in an instant : 75 modern recipes for your pressure
    cooker, slow cooker, and Instant Pot®/ Melissa Clark.
Description: New York : Clarkson Potter, 2017. | Trademark sign
    appears after Pot in title.
Identifiers: LCCN 2017021737 (print) | LCCN 2017022838 (ebook)
    | ISBN 9781524762971 (Ebook) | ISBN 9781524762964
    (hardback)
Subjects: LCSH: Quick and easy cooking. | BISAC: COOKING /
    Methods / Special Appliances. | COOKING / Methods / Slow
    Cooking. | COOKING / Methods / Quick & Easy. | LCGFT:
    Cookbooks.
Classification: LCC TX833.5 (ebook) | LCC TX833.5 .C539 2017
    (print) | DDC 641.5/12—dc23
LC record available at https://lccn.loc.gov2017021737

ISBN 978-1-5247-6296-4
eBook ISBN 978-1-5247-6297-1
Printed in China

Book and cover design by Marysarah Quinn
Cover photography by Christopher Testani
Cook it Slow illustration by Leremy/ Shutterstock
Cook it on the Stove illustration (page 21) by 32 pixels/
Shutterstock

10 9 8 7 6

First Edition

TO DAHLIA AND DANIEL

CONTENTS

YOGURT, CHEESE + EGGS

MEATS

SEAFOOD

INTRODUCTION
WHY I WROTE THIS BOOK

People love their electric pressure cookers with a passion that goes way beyond their feelings for most other kitchen appliances. Having never made it past a friendly acquaintance with my stovetop pressure cooker (currently supporting a colony of dust bunnies in the back of my highest cabinet), I just didn't get it. Why would an electric machine be any different?

If it weren't for an assignment for my column in the *New York Times*, I might not have found out. My task was to see what all the fuss was about. So I bought an electric pressure cooker and went to work.

A mere two hours after the machine was delivered, I was dining on braised beef. But not just any braised beef, some of the best short ribs I'd ever made–spoon-ably tender, deeply flavorful, melt-in-the-mouth luscious. And making them was easier than oven-braising because I didn't have to check the liquid level or turn the meat halfway to ensure even cooking. It was also a heck of a lot faster.

Even better, using the machine wasn't anxiety-provoking in the way of my stove-top model, which carried the baggage of decades of exploding split pea soups.

With an electric pressure cooker, exploding split pea soup just doesn't happen. The latest models are designed with a slew of self-regulating safety features, including sensors to monitor the temperature and amount of pressure inside the unit. All you do is plug it in and tap a button, and it does everything else.

After that happy braised beef experience, I continued putting the machine through its paces, learning its strengths and weaknesses. I wrote the article, and then I kept on going, braising and stewing, making polenta and beans and soups and custards. Once I started, I couldn't stop. Finally, I understood all the love. And now I'm here to share it.

In this book, I focus on the machine's strengths, writing not about what you *can* make in it, but what you *should* make because the electric pressure cooker does it better–faster, or more flavorfully, or with less mess and/or stress. The key to successful pressure cooking is choosing recipes in which softness and succulence is the goal, and which traditionally take hours to get there. It can't cook a whole chicken very well, and it doesn't do crisp or crunchy. So don't ask it to and you won't be disappointed.

Instead, try braising some pork shoulder with olives and fennel (page 56) until it collapses into a gorgeous brawny mound over a bed of buttery polenta (page 93). Perfect your chili (page 38) or chicken and dumplings (page 58), or take on a tahdig–herbed Persian rice with a golden, buttery crust. Or try your hand at the best crème brûlée imaginable (page 150), flavored with fresh mint or vanilla bean, to awe your friends and family.

I hope this book and the pot itself will inspire you in the kitchen. Enjoy it. Play with it. I promise, your split pea soup will not end up on the ceiling, but on the table for all to savor.

RECIPE KEY
LOOK FOR THESE ICONS THROUGHOUT THE BOOK:
GF **GLUTEN-FREE**
P **PALEO**
V **VEGAN**
VEG **VEGETARIAN**

GETTING TO KNOW YOUR
ELECTRIC PRESSURE COOKER

If you've just bought an electric pressure cooker, you're all set to dive into a whole new and thrilling world of cooking that's fast, easy, and highly convenient—once you learn how to use your new machine. If you're an old hand at this, you can skip this section. But novices should read on for some crucial information that will help you avoid the pitfalls and get comfortable with all the functions of your device.

First, some terminology. Most electric pressure cookers are also multipurpose cookers, or multipots, meaning they can do many things beyond just cooking your dinner under pressure. Most models have a similar variety of functions: you can steam, sauté, slow-cook, pressure-cook, and even make yogurt with some brands.

The pressure function is one of the handiest because by cooking foods at a lower temperature but higher pressure, it allows for a faster cooking time than you would need on the stove or in the oven. It lets you achieve certain shortcuts, like cooking dried beans without soaking them first or cooking polenta without stirring. And it is amazing for braising meats, which never dry out and always cook up tender and luscious.

In terms of convenience, an electric pressure cooker is a lot like the slow cooker except that it gets your dinner on the table a day or so faster. Just throw your food in and go do

something else. It will be there when you're ready for it.

Because I'm always in a rush, and assume you usually are too, I've written most of these recipes to use the pressure cooker function whenever possible. This gets your dinner on the table in the quickest way.

But whenever the results are equally good using the slow cooker function, I have included directions for that as well (see "Cook It Slow" at the end of some of the recipes). This gives you options. Because sometimes you do need to slow things down to make them fit most easily into your schedule. The choice is yours.

Note that these recipes will work in any electric pressure cooker on the market. In terms of developing the recipes, I tested them using three popular brands: Instant Pot, Breville, and Fagor, and found them all more or less the same in terms of functionality. They all cooked the ingredients pretty similarly. The differences were in their designs. Some models were more intuitive for me to use than others. This, however, is entirely subjective. Do some research before you buy if you don't yet own a pot. In general, though, unless you're regularly feeding eight or more people, a 6-quart machine is perfectly fine. However, if you're cooking for larger crowds, you might consider the 8-quart size.

PRESSURE COOKER PARTS

It's imperative that you read the manual for your electric pressure cooker before you use it the first time, because the brands vary a bit. However, most pressure cookers come with the following parts:

- **Lid with steam valve and pressure valve**
- **Outer body**
- **Inner pot**
- **Steamer rack or basket**
- **Condensation reservoir** (for condensation during slow cooking; it attaches at the side of the lid once it's closed)

About the steam valve: This valve allows the pressure cooker to either build pressure or release it. It has a sealing (locked) position and a venting (open) position. When pressure-cooking, the valve must be in the sealing position. (Consult your manual if your valve looks different or has other options.)

About the pressure valve: This metal valve indicates when the cooker is pressurized and when it is not. When the cooker reaches pressure, it will pop up. When the pressure is released, it will drop down. In some models, the valve might be hidden underneath a cover. But it's there doing its job whether you see it or not.

MULTICOOKER FUNCTIONS

Consult the manual for the specific instructions on how to operate each of these functions in your particular multicooker.

Most electric pressure cookers have the following functions: sauté, pressure cook, and slow cook. Some also have a yogurt setting. These are the four main functions that are used in this book. You can experiment with other settings your cooker might have (rice, beans, poultry, steam, for example) when you're not following a recipe. Those settings are pre-programmed with the amount of time and pressure level needed for *most* bean, rice, poultry, etc. preparations. But what you gain in ease you lose in terms of control. After all, there may be only one chicken setting, but what if you're using all dark or all light meat? The cooking times for those are different, so you will want to experiment. For this book, I have fine-tuned the recipes to give you the best possible results based on my extensive testing with the most popular multicookers.

Sauté: The sauté function works like a burner on your stove, heating the inner pot from the bottom up and allowing you to brown meats and vegetables and to simmer sauces to reduce them. The sauté function on most cookers has several levels from low to high (check your manual to find out) so you can adjust the heat. If yours doesn't, and if at some point the pot seems too hot and the food is turning too dark too quickly, simply turn the machine off for a few minutes to bring the heat down. Then turn it back on if necessary. It's not a perfect solution but it works well enough, and the pot will adjust to the temperature change (on or off) fairly quickly. Or you can always brown the ingredients in a skillet on top of the stove and then transfer them to the pot for the remainder of the cooking. Note that when sautéing, the lid of the pressure cooker should always be off.

Pressure Cook: There are two options for pressure cooking: high and low. Check the recipe and set the cooker for the correct pressure level; then set the length of time you'd like the ingredients to cook. High pressure is used for most recipes, with low pressure appropriate for more delicate ingredients, like seafood, custards, some vegetables and eggs.

Slow Cook: If you have already used a Crock-Pot or other slow cooker, this will be familiar to you: the slow cooker function on your multicooker cooks your food very, very slowly. You may have the option to cook it at either a high or low setting, depending on your model. Some models provide a separate clear glass cover so you can monitor the food as it is slow-cooking. Other models will have you lock the lid on as if you were going to pressure-cook the dish—except, crucially, that the steam valve is open so the steam can vent. And you can take the top off to check on things as they cook.

Yogurt: The use of this function will vary based on the recipe and your model. Most yogurt functions will heat the pot to between 180° and 200°F, which is the temperature needed for the milk to ferment. The nice thing about the yogurt function is that you don't have to worry about the milk burning or bubbling over, and you can be sure it always reaches the correct temperature. Nor do you have to worry about finding a warm but not too warm spot for the yogurt to ferment. The multipot takes care of that for you. Consult your manual for exact instructions.

WHAT YOU'RE GOING TO NEED FOR THESE RECIPES

- **Aluminum foil,** for covering pans and for making slings (see page 15)
- **Metal springform cake pan:** 6- or 7-inch (never put any glass cookware in the multicooker)
- **Soufflé dish (porcelain):** 1-quart dish and 1½- or 2-quart dish (all about 7 inches in diameter)
- **Ramekins (porcelain):** 4 to 6 ounces each
- **Variety of steamer baskets and steamer racks:** Most pressure cookers will come

with at least one steamer rack. This sits at the bottom of the pressure cooker, usually over water or some kind of liquid. Some racks have attached metal handles, which allow you to lower and lift soufflé dishes and cake pans from the pot without tipping the dish. You'll want at least one steamer rack; if yours does not have a handle, you can simply make a foil sling to help you lower it into, and lift it up from, the pot (see page 15).

I'd also advise you to get at least one steamer basket. Different from a rack, this contraption has short legs and a basket-like top with a handle. It's handy for lifting a lot of small things out of the pressure cooker at one time—potatoes, for example—which would roll off a flat steamer rack.

NOTES FOR PRESSURE COOKING:
MANUAL VERSUS NATURAL RELEASE

- When the pressure-cooking time is up, the cooker will automatically change to the "keep warm" function and begin to gradually lose pressure. It can take as long as 30 minutes to release naturally on its own. If the recipe calls for an immediate manual release, turn the steam valve to its venting position. When the cook time is complete take care to keep your hand away from the valve (not above it) so as not to burn yourself when the rush of hot steam blasts forth. Some people like to turn the valve with the handle of a wooden spoon. Or consider covering the valve with a dish towel before opening it, which has the added bonus of keeping the steam from spraying all over your kitchen. I usually use my hands, albeit carefully, approaching the valve from the side rather than the top.

- Note that if a recipe calls for a manual pressure release, it's important to do as suggested as soon as the machine beeps (or set a timer if you're going to be in another room). Otherwise the food inside might overcook.

* Some recipes call for a specific time for natural release before manually releasing the rest of the pressure. In that case, turn off the pot if it doesn't turn itself off but do not release the valve until the natural release time has passed. Then open the steam valve to release the rest of the pressure. This allows the food to continue to cook a little longer than with a straight manual release, but without the pot being on full pressure for that whole time. It's a slightly gentler and slower cooking environment.

- The time for a full natural release varies (usually between 10 and 20 minutes, but it can be longer). The longer the pressure cooker has been on, the longer the natural release will take. On most models you will know that all the pressure has released naturally when the pressure valve drops down. Or if your valve is covered and you can't see it, feel the top of the lid; it should be lukewarm but not hot.

A note on reaching pressure: When you select pressure cooking and set a time, the clock will not immediately begin to count down. This is because the pot must first build pressure before it starts to cook. This can take anywhere from 3 to 10 minutes depending upon the contents of the pot. Always double-check that the steam valve is in the locked, sealing position. Pressure cannot build if it is venting.

A note on pressure cooking versus slow cooking: In this book, I include the cook time for both pressure cooking and slow cooking when applicable. The initial directions will be those for pressure cooking. Following the recipe, there will be directions for "Cook It Slow." If you prefer to cook a dish all day long or overnight, the slow cooking option will be useful for you.

- Tongs are helpful for lifting out small hot pans, ramekins, or dishes. I usually use them in one hand with oven mitts in the other hand.

- If your steamer rack does not have handles, it's easy to build a sling that will help you lift soufflé dishes and cake pans out of the cooker. To make one, fold a long (about 16 inches) piece of aluminum foil into thirds so that it can sit under the dish or pan and extend up the sides of the pressure cooker pot (as handles). This will help you lift and lower the dish or pan from the cooker. Be sure to leave the sling in the machine while cooking so you can use it to lift the dish out afterward. Note that it will be hot after cooking, so use oven mitts.

MORE TIPS

- Lock the steam valve before pressure cooking. Pressure will never build if the valve is turned to venting.
- The steam valve should NOT be locked when steaming, slow cooking, or using the yogurt function. The entire lid should be off when sautéing.
- Don't fill the pot more than two-thirds full with any liquid or stew. Keep in mind that some foods expand, for example rice or oats.
- The condensation collector should be attached for slow cooking to prevent water from leaking onto your counter.

- Always cover cake pans and soufflé dishes with aluminum foil when cooking under pressure. Without the foil, condensation will collect in the dishes and water down the food, in some cases ruining it (puddings and custards, for example).
- To avoid being burned and to avoid having your kitchen fill with steam, you can put a dish towel over the steamer valve before releasing the pressure manually. Do not hold your hands directly over the steam valve.

- Be aware that when the lid is removed after the pressure is released, there will be some excess water clinging to it. Turn the lid outward and away from you, so that the condensation does not drip back into the pot.
- If something comes out undercooked, re-cover the pot, lock the steam valve, re-pressurize, and cook again for an extra few minutes (depending on how much more time you think the dish needs). If the recipe initially called for a natural release, release it naturally again.

YOGURT, CHEESE

+

EGGS

PLAIN YOGURT

TIME: 9 HOURS, PLUS 8 HOURS CHILLING

YIELD: 7 CUPS

GF · VEG

---

2 quarts whole milk, preferably organic

½ cup heavy cream (optional)

2 tablespoons plain yogurt (look for the words "active cultures" on the label)

NOTE: To make Greek yogurt, after you've let the yogurt chill for 8 hours or overnight (step 3), spoon it into a cheesecloth-lined colander set in a bowl, and let it drain until it reaches the consistency you like, anywhere from 1 hour to 4 hours. Save the whey that drains out and use the milky, tangy liquid in smoothies, soups, breads, and other recipes. It's great as a substitute for water when making lemonade. And I sometimes use half whey and half stock in the Red Lentil Soup with Mint Oil (page 122). Whey can be frozen for up to 3 months and is full of protein, B vitamins, and calcium.

Serve your yogurt over fruit and/or granola, use it to make savory yogurt sauces, or drizzle it with honey or maple syrup for a little added sweetness.

Once you start making your own yogurt, it's hard to go back to store-bought. Homemade is not only fresher and much less expensive, it's also incredibly easy—and made even easier with an electric pressure cooker that has a yogurt setting. You can use low-fat milk here instead of whole milk if you like, but skim milk doesn't work very well, tending to yield yogurt that's quite thin. Sheep and goat milk will also work if you have a source for them, with sheep milk being extremely rich and sweet tasting, while goat milk is tangier and a little more earthy. And unless making a lower-fat yogurt is your goal, don't omit the cream. It really adds richness in both flavor and texture.

---

1. Heat the milk: Pour the milk, and cream if using, into the pressure cooker and cover it (the steam valve should be turned to "pressure" or "sealing." Select the yogurt function (in the Instant Pot, the screen will light up indicating "boil"; if you have a different machine, consult your manual, and heat the milk to 180°F, about 26 minutes (in the Instant Pot, "Yogt" will appear on the screen when the milk reaches that temperature). Uncover, being careful to avoid letting condensation on lid drip into the milk. Keep milk at 180°F for 5 minutes by turning the yogurt function on again, with the pot uncovered. This helps thicken it.

2. Cool the milk: Turn off or unplug your pressure cooker, remove the metal basin, and transfer it to a wire rack. Let it cool until the milk reaches 115°F, 35 to 40 minutes. You can speed up the process by placing the basin in an ice bath (I fill my sink with water and ice and set the basin in that). The milk will develop a thin top skin; just give it a stir once it has cooled.

3. Add the starter culture: In a medium bowl, stir together the active yogurt and ½ cup of the warm milk from the pressure cooker basin. Then stir the yogurt mixture into the rest of the milk, and place the basin back inside the pressure cooker. Cover, and set the steam valve to "venting." Select the yogurt function, and then use the "+" button to add 8 hours. Once finished, the Instant Pot will read "Yogt." Remove the lid and ladle the yogurt into containers. Seal the containers and refrigerate for at least 8 hours or overnight, and up to 1 week.

SOY MILK YOGURT

TIME: 12 TO 14 HOURS

YIELD: 3½ CUPS

GF • V • VEG

___

32 ounces soy milk (containing only soy and filtered water)

2 tablespoons store-bought nondairy yogurt

___

You can use any nondairy yogurt as the culture for this recipe. Soy and coconut yogurts are the easiest to find. Look for shelf-stable soy milk—the refrigerated kind usually contains thickeners and sweeteners. Serve this with honey or your favorite jam stirred in, or over a bowl of ripe fresh fruit.

___

1. Stir together the soy milk and store-bought yogurt in the pressure cooker. Cover, and turn on the yogurt function, set for 12 hours with the steam vent open.

2. After 12 hours, taste the yogurt. If you want it tangier, let it go for up to an additional 2 hours (14 hours total).

3. Stir the yogurt well, transfer it to sealed containers, and refrigerate for at least 6 hours and up to 5 days (the yogurt will thicken as it chills).

FRESH COCONUT YOGURT

TIME: 24 HOURS

YIELD: 3½ CUPS

GF • VEG

---

2 13.5-ounce cans full-fat organic coconut milk (not refrigerated nondairy beverage)

2 tablespoons store-bought nondairy yogurt

Meat from 1 young coconut (optional)

Using coconut milk instead of regular milk will give you a sweet-tart, albeit thin-textured, yogurt. For something thicker, you can puree the yogurt with the meat of a fresh young coconut. Fresh young coconuts (not to be confused with mature coconuts with the brown husks) are becoming more available at Whole Foods and other specialty markets, large supermarkets, and Asian markets (don't try to substitute coconut flakes or chips—they don't work). Be sure to use canned coconut milk here, not refrigerated coconut nondairy beverages or creamers, which are laden with stabilizers. You can use any nondairy yogurt, either coconut or soy, as the starter here.

---

1. Stir together the coconut milk and store-bought yogurt in the pressure cooker. Then cover it and turn on the yogurt function, set for 24 hours with the steam vent open.

2. After 24 hours, stir it gently. At this point, you can transfer the yogurt to a sealed container and refrigerate it; the yogurt will be thin and will thicken up a bit as it chills. However, if you want an even thicker yogurt, transfer half of the yogurt to a blender and process it with the coconut meat; then stir in the remaining yogurt and transfer the yogurt to a sealed container. Either way, the yogurt will keep in the refrigerator for up to 5 days.

HOMEMADE RICOTTA

TIME: 35 MINUTES

YIELD: ABOUT 1½ CUPS

GF · VEG

**6 cups whole milk
(use the best quality milk
you can get)**

¾ cup heavy cream

2 tablespoons white vinegar

½ teaspoon fine sea salt (optional)

COOK IT ON THE STOVE

To cook this in a regular saucepan, bring
the milk, cream, and vinegar to a boil in a
pot on the stove. Simmer for 1 to 2 minutes,
until curds form. Then follow the
directions in steps 2 and 3.

Homemade ricotta is one of the easiest and most delicious
things you can make. You'll need to use an electric pressure cooker that has a yogurt or boil setting because the
milk has to boil in order to separate into curds. (You can
also make this in a pot on the stove; see note below.)

This recipe will result in a small amount of excellent
creamy ricotta and a lot of tangy whey, which is the by-
product. Don't throw the whey out! It's high in protein,
B vitamins, and calcium and excellent in soups, dips,
smoothies, and baked goods. It will last in the fridge for
about a week, and even freezes well for up to 3 months.

I prefer my ricotta unsalted, but you can add the salt if
you like.

---

1. Pour the milk and cream into an electric pressure cooker,
cover it with the vent left open, press the yogurt function,
and adjust it to "boil" (see your pressure cooker manual if
your yogurt function works differently). When the pressure
cooker beeps, turn it off, remove the cover, take the pot out
of the pressure cooker, and set it on a heat-proof surface.
Stir in the vinegar and let the mixture sit until curds form,
about 2 minutes.

2. Once curds have formed, stir in the salt, if using, and
then pour the mixture through a large cheesecloth-
lined fine-mesh sieve set over a bowl (the bowl will catch
the whey).

3. Let the sieve sit for 5 to 15 minutes, depending on how
thick you like your ricotta (the longer it sits, the thicker it
will be). The ricotta will keep, covered and refrigerated,
for up to 5 days.

EGGS COOKED
HARD OR SOFT

TIME: 10 MINUTES

YIELD: VARIABLE

GF • P • VEG

___

Large eggs, as many as you like

___

Cooking eggs in your pressure cooker isn't any faster than using a regular pot on the stove. The benefit lies in the peeling. Pressure-cooked eggs in the shell are a dream to peel; the shells slip off easily without nicking the whites. You can adjust the cooking time to get either soft- or hard-cooked eggs. Note that the times listed below are for large eggs. If your eggs are extra-large or jumbo, you might have to add an extra 30 seconds to a minute before you release the pressure. Smaller eggs might take less time. Experiment to find what's exactly right for your taste, your eggs, and your particular model of pressure cooker. It's not an exact science.

___

1. Fill a bowl with ice water and place it next to your pressure cooker.

2. Fill the pressure cooker with 1 cup of water and insert the steamer rack. Place the eggs on the rack, forming a pyramid if you're cooking a lot of them.

3. Cook on low pressure for 5 to 8 minutes. Five minutes gives you very runny-centered yolks (think soft-boiled). Eight minutes gives you light-colored, firmly set hard-cooked eggs. Six to seven minutes gives you dark, moist yolks that can be slightly soft (but not runny).

4. Release the pressure manually; then use tongs to transfer the eggs to the bowl of ice water. Let them sit for a few minutes before peeling. The eggs will still be a little warm if you peel them after 2 minutes. For chilled eggs, let them sit for 5 to 10 minutes and then peel them.

SHAKSHUKA
WITH HERBED YOGURT SAUCE

TIME: 30 MINUTES

YIELD: 4 SERVINGS

GF · VEG

---

3 tablespoons extra-virgin olive oil

1 large onion, halved and
thinly sliced

1 large red bell pepper,
seeded and thinly sliced

4 garlic cloves: 3 thinly sliced,
1 grated on a Microplane or minced

1 teaspoon ground cumin

1 teaspoon sweet paprika

⅛ teaspoon cayenne pepper,
or to taste

1 28-ounce can whole plum tomatoes
with their juices, coarsely chopped

¾ teaspoon salt,
plus more as needed

¼ teaspoon freshly ground black pepper,
plus more as needed

4 extra-large eggs

½ cup plain whole-milk yogurt

½ cup finely chopped fresh herbs,
such as parsley, cilantro, dill,
or a mixture

Hot sauce, for serving (optional)

This Middle Eastern dish of simmered tomatoes, peppers, and onions with runny eggs is just as good for dinner as it is for brunch. The yogurt sauce adds a cooling herbal note that's not traditional but is utterly delightful. The list of ingredients may seem long, but once you've got them assembled, the dish comes together fairly quickly. And it's worth making if you love savory egg dishes.

---

1. Using the sauté function, heat the oil in the pressure cooker. Stir in the onion and bell pepper, and cook until they are starting to soften, about 5 minutes. Stir in the sliced garlic, cumin, paprika, and cayenne, and cook for 1 minute. Pour in the tomatoes, and season with the ¾ teaspoon salt and ¼ teaspoon pepper. Cover and cook on high pressure for 5 minutes. Manually release the pressure.

2. Use the back of a spoon to make 4 indents in the tomato sauce, and then gently crack the eggs into the indents; season to taste with salt and pepper. Cover and cook on low pressure for 1 minute.

3. Meanwhile, make the yogurt sauce: In a small bowl, combine the yogurt, grated garlic, and salt to taste. Stir in the chopped herbs.

4. Release the pressure manually. If you prefer your eggs with a firmer yolk, put the cover back on the pot and let it sit for 2 to 5 minutes to cook in the residual heat. Spoon the eggs and sauce into bowls for serving. Top with the herb yogurt, and a dash of hot sauce if desired.

STEEL-CUT OATS
WITH MAPLE SYRUP + CURRANTS

TIME: 35 MINUTES
YIELD: 4 TO 6 SERVINGS
VEG

---

1 tablespoon unsalted butter, plus more for serving

1 cup steel-cut oats

¼ cup dried currants

1 tablespoon maple syrup, plus more for serving

¼ teaspoon kosher salt

Flaky sea salt, for serving (optional)

COOK IT SLOW

Cook on high for 5 to 7 hours or low for 8 to 10 hours.

I prefer to cook my oatmeal without any milk, with just water, and then to add a big dollop of butter or a drizzle of heavy cream to the bowl before serving. I feel I get a deeper oat flavor that way, which contrasts with the creaminess of the topping. In this recipe, I also sauté the oats in butter and maple syrup before adding the liquid. It brings out their nutty character and adds just a light touch of sweetness that you can augment with more syrup when serving. Feel free to substitute raisins or chopped dried cherries or apricots for the currants. Or omit entirely.

Be sure to use steel-cut oats (also called Irish oats) in this recipe. Rolled oats would turn to mush if you cooked them for this long under pressure.

---

1. Using the sauté function, melt the butter in the pressure cooker. Then stir in the oats, currants, syrup, and salt; stir until the oats are toasted and fragrant, about 3 minutes.

2. Stir in 3¼ cups water, cover, and cook on high pressure for 10 minutes. Let the pressure release naturally for 10 minutes; then release the remaining pressure manually. Serve with additional maple syrup, butter, and a sprinkling of flaky sea salt if desired.

EGGS
WITH SPINACH, SMOKED SALMON + PICKLED SHALLOTS

TIME: 30 MINUTES

YIELD: 4 SERVINGS

GF • VEG (WITHOUT THE SALMON)

———————

2 teaspoons sherry vinegar

½ teaspoon sugar

Kosher salt

2 shallots, thinly sliced

4 tablespoons (½ stick)
unsalted butter

20 ounces (about 4 quarts) baby spinach,
large stems removed

1 cup chopped fresh dill,
plus more for serving

½ cup heavy cream

Freshly ground black pepper

4 large eggs, cold from the fridge

2 to 4 ounces smoked salmon

Crème fraîche, for serving
(optional)

———————

In this company-worthy brunch dish, eggs are nestled in a bed of creamed spinach flecked with dill, then cooked under low pressure until the whites are set but the yolks are still runny. Smoked salmon makes an elegant garnish, but if you're going for a more modest—or vegetarian—dish, you can leave it out. The mingling of egg yolk, cream, spinach, and the garnish of pickled shallots is satisfying even without the fish.

———————

1. In a small bowl, combine the vinegar, sugar, a pinch of salt, and the shallots. Let the mixture sit while you prepare the spinach and eggs.

2. Using the sauté function, melt the butter in the pressure cooker. Then stir in the spinach in batches and cook until wilted, about 5 minutes. Stir in the dill, cream, and ½ teaspoon salt, and continue to cook until the liquid has almost evaporated, 12 to 15 minutes. Add the pepper, taste, and add more salt if needed.

3. Turn off the sauté function, and use the back of a spoon to make 4 divots in the spinach. Crack the eggs into the divots, cover the pressure cooker, and cook on low pressure for 1 minute. Release the steam manually. If the eggs are less cooked than you like, cover the pot again and let it sit for 1 to 3 minutes longer to let the eggs cook in the residual heat of the pot. Transfer the eggs, in their beds of spinach, to serving plates. Drape them with the salmon, sprinkle with the shallots and extra dill, and dollop with crème fraîche if you like. Serve immediately.

LEEK + ARTICHOKE
FRITTATA

TIME: 1 HOUR
YIELD: 4 SERVINGS
VEG

———

**1 tablespoon unsalted butter,
plus more for the soufflé dish**

**5 tablespoons grated
Parmesan cheese**

1 tablespoon extra-virgin olive oil

**2 small leeks (white and light green parts
only), halved and thinly sliced**

**1 teaspoon kosher salt,
plus more as needed**

½ cup milk

2 tablespoons all-purpose flour

9 large eggs

**1 tablespoon finely chopped
fresh basil or parsley**

**½ teaspoon finely chopped
fresh thyme**

**¼ teaspoon freshly ground
black pepper**

**¾ cup (about 2 ounces) shredded
Gruyère cheese**

**⅓ cup marinated artichoke hearts,
drained and coarsely chopped**

———

Use this recipe as a template for creating any variety of pressure cooker frittata you like, changing up the vegetables and cheese to suit your taste and what you have on hand. Shallots, scallions, or onion can stand in for the leeks. Any cooked vegetable can be substituted for the artichokes. So if you were wondering what to do with that small amount of leftover sautéed spinach or roasted butternut squash, here's the perfect place.

Taste your artichokes before using. Some brands are acidic. If yours is, rinse before using.

———

1. Butter a 1½-quart soufflé dish and dust the sides with 2 tablespoons of the Parmesan. Set it aside.

2. Using the sauté function, heat the 1 tablespoon butter and the oil in the pressure cooker. Stir in the leeks and ¼ teaspoon of the salt, and cook, stirring often and lowering the heat if necessary (and possible) to prevent burning, until golden brown, 5 to 10 minutes.

3. Meanwhile, in a large bowl, whisk together the milk and flour. Then whisk in the eggs, basil, thyme, remaining ¾ teaspoon salt, pepper, and Gruyère.

4. Turn off the heat and stir the artichokes into the leeks. Then mix the leek mixture into the egg mixture. Scrape that mixture into the prepared soufflé dish. Cover it with aluminum foil.

5. Pour 1½ cups water into the pressure cooker. You can either place a steamer rack in the bottom of the pot and then lower the soufflé dish onto the rack using a homemade sling (see page 15), or, if you have a rack with an attached handle, lower the rack and dish all at once. Cover and cook on high pressure for 16 minutes.

6. Allow the pressure to release naturally for 10 minutes, and then release the remaining pressure manually. Using oven mitts, remove the soufflé dish from the pressure cooker. Remove the foil.

7. Heat the broiler. Sprinkle the remaining 3 tablespoons Parmesan over the frittata, and broil until it is golden brown, 1 to 2 minutes. Let it sit for 5 minutes before serving.

MEATS

GARLICKY CUBAN PORK

TIME: 2½ HOURS, PLUS 1 HOUR
MARINATING
YIELD: 8 TO 10 SERVINGS
GF (USING CORN TORTILLAS)

---

8 garlic cloves

Juice of 1 grapefruit (about ⅔ cup)

Finely grated zest and juice
of 1 lime

3 tablespoons extra-virgin olive oil

2 tablespoons light brown sugar

1 tablespoon fresh oregano leaves

2 teaspoons ground cumin

1½ tablespoons kosher salt,
plus more to taste

1 4- to 5-pound boneless pork shoulder,
cut into 4 pieces

1 bay leaf

Chopped fresh cilantro leaves,
for serving

Lime wedges, for serving

Hot sauce, for serving

Tortillas, for serving (optional)

Fresh tomato salsa, for serving
(optional)

This cumin-scented, garlic-laced pork is marinated with grapefruit, lime, and fresh oregano for a flavor that's earthy and garlicky, yet bright from the citrus. The meat itself is as tender as can be, falling to shreds with the touch of a fork. Serve it over Garlic Rice (page 85) for a soft bed with maximum pungency. Or tuck it into tortillas along with some salsa and avocado to create tacos.

---

1. In a blender or mini food processor, combine the garlic, grapefruit juice, lime zest and juice, 2 tablespoons of the oil, brown sugar, oregano, cumin, and salt; process until blended. Transfer to a large bowl and add the pork and bay leaf; toss to combine. Marinate, covered, at room temperature for 1 hour (or refrigerate for up to 6 hours).

2. Using the sauté function set on high if available, heat the remaining 1 tablespoon oil in the pressure cooker (or use a large skillet). Remove the pork from the marinade, reserving the marinade, and shake the meat to remove any excess liquid. Cook until it is browned on all sides, about 12 minutes (you will need to do this in batches, transferring the browned pork pieces to a plate as you go).

3. When all the pork is browned, return the pieces to the pot along with any juices from the plate. (If you used a skillet, add 1 tablespoon water and use a wooden spoon to scrape the skillet well to include all the browned bits stuck to the bottom.) Add the reserved marinade to the pot. Cover and cook on high pressure for 80 minutes. Let the pressure release naturally.

4. Remove the pork from the cooking liquid (jus). Taste the jus, and if it seems bland or too thin, boil it down either in the pressure cooker on the sauté setting or in a separate pot on the stove until it thickens slightly and intensifies in flavor, 7 to 15 minutes. Remove the bay leaf and add a bit of salt if necessary. If you'd like to degrease the jus, use a fat separator to do so, or just let the jus settle and spoon the fat off the top.

5. Shred the meat, using your hands or two forks. Toss the meat with the jus to taste (be generous—1½ to 2 cups should do it), and serve with cilantro, lime wedges, and hot sauce.

STICKY TAMARIND
BABY BACK
RIBS

TIME: 1 HOUR 15 MINUTES
YIELD: 4 SERVINGS

---

4 to 5 pounds baby back ribs

**1 teaspoon kosher salt,
plus more to taste**

¼ cup tamarind paste or concentrate

**¼ cup fresh orange juice
(from about ½ orange)**

¼ cup honey, plus more as needed

2 tablespoons soy sauce

¼ teaspoon grated lime zest

1 tablespoon fresh lime juice

1 star anise pod

**2 tablespoons neutral oil,
such as safflower or canola**

**4 small shallots, diced
(about ⅓ cup)**

**1½ teaspoons grated peeled
fresh ginger**

**2 garlic cloves, grated on a
Microplane or minced**

COOK IT SLOW

Add ¾ cup water to the slow cooker when adding the sauce in step 4. Cook the ribs on high for 4 to 5 hours or on low for 6 to 8 hours. Remove the ribs, reduce the sauce, and broil as described in step 6.

These gingery sweet-and-sour glazed ribs are tender and intensely flavored—and pretty much impossible to stop eating once you start. The sauce also works well on spare-ribs if you'd like to substitute those here. Just reduce the cooking time by a few minutes on the pressure setting, or as much as an hour if using the slow cooker setting.

---

1. Cut the ribs into chunks of 2 or 3 ribs, depending on their size, and place them in a large bowl. Toss with the 1 teaspoon salt, and set aside while you prepare the sauce.

2. In a small bowl, combine the tamarind, orange juice, honey, soy sauce, lime zest and juice, and star anise. Set aside.

3. Using the sauté function, heat the oil in the pressure cooker. Stir in the shallots and cook until they are starting to brown, about 5 minutes. Stir in the ginger and garlic and cook until fragrant, another minute; then stir in the tamarind mixture. Bring to a simmer, and then scrape the sauce into the large bowl of ribs. Toss gently to combine.

4. Arrange the ribs standing up along the outer edge of the pressure cooker, making a ring with the meat side of the ribs facing out. Continue with the remaining ribs, arranging them to make concentric circles. Pour any remaining sauce over the ribs, cover, and cook on high pressure for 32 minutes. Allow the pressure to release naturally.

5. Heat the broiler.

6. Transfer the ribs, meat-side down, to a rimmed baking sheet. Turn the pressure cooker to the sauté function and cook to reduce the sauce until it's thick, about 15 minutes; spoon the fat off the top when finished. Taste the sauce, and adjust the seasoning or add more honey if necessary; then brush the ribs with the sauce. Broil the ribs until they are charred in spots, 1 to 3 minutes. Then flip them over, brush with more sauce, and broil on that side until charred. Serve immediately, with more sauce on the side.

CLASSIC BEEF + BEAN CHILI

TIME: 2 HOURS

YIELD: 8 SERVINGS

———

1 pound dried pinto beans, rinsed

2¾ teaspoons salt, plus more as needed

1 bay leaf

2 to 4 tablespoons bacon fat, olive oil, or other oil, as needed

2 pounds ground beef

2 large Spanish onions, diced (4 cups)

2 poblano chiles or 1 large green bell pepper, seeded and diced

1 large red or orange bell pepper, seeded and diced

5 garlic cloves: 4 chopped, 1 grated on a Microplane or minced

2 to 3 jalapeño peppers, seeded and minced

3 to 4 tablespoons New Mexico chile powder

2 teaspoons dried oregano, crumbled

2 teaspoons ground cumin

1 teaspoon freshly ground black pepper

½ teaspoon ground coriander

1 small bunch fresh cilantro, leaves and stems separated and chopped

¼ cup beer (nothing too bitter; pilsners and lagers work better than ales)

26 to 28 ounces diced canned (or boxed) tomatoes and their juices

Chopped onion or sliced scallions, for serving

Hot sauce, to taste

———

Spicy but not fiery, hearty and very satisfying, this is a chili recipe you'll make again and again. Because the vegetables are sautéed in stages so that their flavors build upon one another, it does take a fair amount of work. But its complexity is well worth the effort. You can substitute other ground meat for the beef here. Dark-meat turkey, pork, and lamb all work well. Or use a combination. Note that chili is always best served the next day, and will thicken considerably in the fridge overnight. Keep this in mind when deciding whether to simmer it at the end.

———

1. Place the beans, 1¼ teaspoons of the salt, the bay leaf, and 6 cups of water in the electric pressure cooker, cover, and cook on high pressure for 30 minutes. Let the pressure release naturally. The beans should be cooked through; if not, return to high pressure for another 5 minutes.

2. While the beans are cooking, brown the meat and vegetables: Heat a large skillet over medium-high heat, and then add 2 tablespoons of the bacon fat. When it's hot, add half of the beef and ¾ teaspoon of the salt and sauté until the meat is well browned all over, about 5 minutes. Use a slotted spoon to transfer the beef to a large bowl. Repeat with the remaining beef and salt, adding more oil if needed.

3. If the skillet looks dry, add a little more oil to it. Add the onions and sauté until they are pale gold and limp, about 10 minutes. Add the chiles and bell pepper and a pinch of salt, and sauté until the peppers are tender and the onions bronzed, 10 minutes longer. Transfer the vegetables to the bowl containing the beef.

4. If the skillet looks dry, add a little more oil. Sauté the chopped garlic and jalapeños until fragrant and tender, 1 to 2 minutes; then add the chile powder, oregano, cumin, black pepper, and coriander. Add the cilantro stems, saving the leaves for garnish. Sauté until the chile powder darkens, 1 minute. Pour in the beer and let it reduce, scraping up the browned bits on the bottom of the pan, 2 minutes. Add the tomatoes and let simmer until thickened, 5 to 7 minutes.

5. When the beans are done, add the beef and vegetables, and the tomato mixture, to the beans and their liquid in the pressure cooker pot. Cook on high pressure for 30 minutes. Allow the pressure to release naturally. If the mixture is too thin, simmer it on the sauté function for a few minutes to reduce the liquid. Stir in the grated garlic and chopped cilantro leaves. Serve garnished with the onions and hot sauce to taste.

COOK IT SLOW

Cook the beans on high for 4 to 5 hours. Then add the browned meat, vegetables, and tomato mixture and continue to cook on high for another 3 to 4 hours or on low for another 5 to 6 hours.

KOREAN CHILE-BRAISED BRISKET
+ KIMCHI COLESLAW

TIME: 2 HOURS 30 MINUTES, PLUS AT
LEAST 1 HOUR MARINATING

YIELD: 8 SERVINGS

————

4 to 5 pounds beef brisket,
cut into 3 or 4 pieces

1 tablespoon dried red chile flakes,
preferably Korean gochugaru

1 tablespoon sweet paprika

2½ teaspoons kosher salt,
plus more to taste

½ teaspoon freshly ground black pepper

1 to 3 tablespoons peanut or safflower oil,
as needed

1 large onion, diced

4 garlic cloves, minced

1 tablespoon grated peeled fresh ginger

1 cup lager-style beer

¼ cup gochujang (Korean chile paste)
or Sriracha

2 tablespoons ketchup

2 tablespoons soy sauce

2 tablespoons light or dark brown sugar

2 teaspoons Asian fish sauce

1 teaspoon toasted sesame oil

Gochujang, a very slightly sweet and powerfully spicy Korean chile paste made from gochugaru (Korean red chile), has become a staple in my kitchen, where it adds a more intense, complex bite than other hot sauces. Here I use it to flavor tender beef brisket, along with the gochugaru chile flakes for added heat, sesame oil, garlic, and lots of fresh ginger. If you can't find gochujang, Sriracha makes a good though slightly less spicy substitute.

And if you're not a coleslaw fan, you can certainly skip it and simply serve some kimchi or a salad on the side.

————

1. Rub the beef with the chile flakes, paprika, salt, and pepper. Cover and refrigerate for 1 hour and up to 24 hours.

2. Set the electric pressure cooker to sauté (or use a large skillet). Add a tablespoon of the oil, let it heat up for a few seconds, and then add a batch of the beef and sear until it's browned all over, about 2 minutes per side, adding more oil as needed. Transfer the beef to a plate and repeat with the remaining batches.

3. If the pot looks dry, add a bit more oil. Add the onion and sauté until golden, 3 to 5 minutes. Add the garlic and ginger and sauté for 1 minute longer. Add the beer, gochujang, ketchup, soy sauce, brown sugar, fish sauce, and sesame oil. Scrape the mixture into the pressure cooker if you have used a skillet. Return beef to the pot.

4. Cover and cook on high pressure for 90 minutes. Let the pressure release naturally for 20 minutes, and then release the remaining pressure manually.

RECIPE CONTINUES

FOR THE KIMCHI COLESLAW

**5 cups shredded cabbage
(from 1 small cabbage)**

**¼ cup chopped kimchi,
plus more to taste**

**2 tablespoons peanut, grapeseed,
or olive oil**

1 teaspoon toasted sesame oil

Juice of ½ lime, plus more to taste

**½ teaspoon fine sea salt,
plus more to taste**

COOK IT SLOW

Cut the beef into 6 to 8 pieces instead of
3 or 4 pieces. Marinate and brown as in
steps 1 and 2. Place the meat in the pot and
cover with the sautéed onion mixture from
step 3. Cook on high for 7 to 9 hours or
low for 10 to 12 hours.

5. To make the kimchi coleslaw, combine the cabbage,
kimchi, both oils, lime juice, and salt in a large bowl and
toss well. Taste, and add more salt or lime juice if needed.

6. Transfer the beef to a plate or a rimmed cutting board
and tent with foil to keep warm. Set the pressure cooker to
sauté and simmer the sauce for 15 to 20 minutes, until it is
reduced by half or two-thirds (remember that it thickens
as it cools). Use a fat separator to skim off the fat, or let the
sauce settle and spoon the fat off the top. Serve the sauce
alongside the beef, with the kimchi coleslaw.

PORT-BRAISED
SHORT RIBS
WITH STAR ANISE

TIME: 2 HOURS,
PLUS AT LEAST 1 HOUR MARINATING
YIELD: 6 SERVINGS

———

4 pounds bone-in beef short ribs

3 bay leaves, torn in half

2½ teaspoons kosher salt

½ teaspoon freshly ground black pepper

5 star anise pods, crumbled

5 garlic cloves: 3 grated on a Microplane, 2 minced

2 tablespoons extra-virgin olive oil

2 leeks, white and light green parts only, thinly sliced

2 carrots, cut into 1-inch chunks

Thumb-size piece of fresh ginger, peeled and cut into ½-inch-thick coins

½ tablespoon all-purpose flour

1 1-inch-wide strip of orange zest (use a vegetable peeler)

½ cup ruby or tawny port wine

½ cup beef or chicken stock, preferably homemade (page 114, or use water)

¼ cup chopped soft herbs (chives, tarragon, basil, parsley, or a combination), for serving

———

COOK IT SLOW

———

Cook on high for 5 to 7 hours or on low for 8 to 10 hours.

Port wine gives these falling-off-the-bone short ribs a gentle winy sweetness while star anise lends a little licorice-like spice. They are intense, meaty, and especially wonderful over a bed of buttery polenta (see page 93). Look for English short ribs, which are cut into large chunks including the bone. They have the best texture for this dish. And if you really hate licorice but love short ribs, you can substitute ¼ teaspoon ground allspice for the star anise.

———

1. Put the short ribs in a bowl and rub them with the bay leaves, 2 teaspoons of the salt, and the pepper, star anise, and grated garlic. Cover and refrigerate for at least 1 hour or preferably overnight.

2. Using the sauté function, set to high if available, heat the oil in the pressure cooker (or do this in a skillet over high heat). In batches, brown the ribs on all sides, 3 to 5 minutes per side, transferring them to a large bowl as they finish (or transfer the ribs to the pressure cooker pot if you browned them in a skillet).

3. Reduce the heat to medium (if your sauté function is not adjustable, unplug the pressure cooker for a few seconds to let it cool down a bit before proceeding). Stir the leeks, carrots, and remaining ½ teaspoon salt into the pressure cooker (or skillet). Cook until the vegetables have softened, about 8 minutes; then stir in the minced garlic, ginger, and flour and cook for 2 more minutes.

4. Stir in the orange zest, port, and stock. Then nestle the ribs back into the pot (or pour the sauce from the skillet over the ribs in the pressure cooker). Cover and cook on high pressure for 40 minutes. Allow the pressure to release naturally.

5. Transfer the ribs to a large bowl, and turn on the sauté function to reduce the liquid left in the cooker until it is thickened and saucy, about 10 minutes. Pour it over the ribs and serve, garnished with the herbs.

JAPANESE
BEEF CURRY

TIME: 1 HOUR 15 MINUTES
YIELD: 4 TO 6 SERVINGS

———

1 tablespoon safflower or grapeseed oil

2 onions, diced

2 pounds beef stew meat,
cut into 1½-inch chunks

2 teaspoons kosher salt

½ teaspoon freshly ground black pepper

2 tablespoons garam masala

3 garlic cloves, grated or minced

1 teaspoon grated peeled fresh ginger

2 large carrots, cut into 1-inch chunks

1 small apple, peeled and grated

1 bay leaf

2 cups chicken, beef, or vegetable stock,
preferably homemade (page 114,
or use water)

1 large sweet potato, peeled and
cut into 1-inch chunks

1 cup sliced shiitake mushrooms
(about 1.5 ounces)

1 bunch fresh mustard greens, leaves
only, coarsely chopped, about 5 cups

3 tablespoons peanut oil

3 tablespoons all-purpose flour

1½ tablespoons ketchup

1 tablespoon Worcestershire sauce

½ tablespoon soy sauce

Cooked white rice, for serving

Toasted sesame oil, for serving

Sesame seeds, for serving

Chopped scallions, for serving

This beef curry is flavored with ginger, shiitakes, and soy sauce, plus apples and a little ketchup for sweetness. It's thick, nuanced, and perfect for spooning over rice (see page 84) for a cozy winter meal. Many similar recipes call for using white potatoes, but I prefer sweet potatoes, which thicken the sauce and add a velvety texture and a little more sweetness.

———

1. Using the sauté function, heat the safflower or grapeseed oil in the pressure cooker. Stir in the onions and cook, stirring often, until caramelized, 15 to 20 minutes.

2. Meanwhile, season the beef with the salt and pepper, and let it sit at room temperature until ready to use.

3. When the onions are dark golden, stir in 1 tablespoon of the garam masala, the garlic, and the ginger, and cook for 1 minute; then stir in the beef, carrots, apple, bay leaf, and stock. Cover and cook on high pressure for 22 minutes, and then manually release the pressure.

4. Stir in the potato and mushrooms, cover, and cook on high pressure for another 3 minutes; then release the pressure manually.

5. Turn on the sauté function, on low if available, and stir in the mustard greens. Let the mixture simmer for a few minutes while you make the roux.

6. To make the roux, heat the peanut oil in a small saucepan over medium heat. Stir in the remaining 1 tablespoon garam masala and the flour, and cook for 2 minutes. Then whisk in the ketchup, Worcestershire sauce, and soy sauce; the roux will become thick and crumbly.

7. Whisk enough of the liquid from the pressure cooker into the roux to make it smooth (about 1 cup), and then scrape the roux into the simmering curry; stir until thickened. Serve with rice, drizzled with sesame oil and garnished with sesame seeds and chopped scallions.

COOK IT SLOW

Cook on high for 5 to 7 hours, adding the potatoes and mushrooms after 2½ hours, or on low for 8 to 10 hours, adding the vegetables after 4 hours. Add the greens and roux on the sauté function as described in steps 5 to 7.

WINE-BRAISED
OXTAILS
WITH FENNEL

TIME: 2 HOURS,
PLUS AT LEAST 1 HOUR MARINATING
YIELD: 6 TO 8 SERVINGS

2½ teaspoons kosher salt,
plus more as needed

2 teaspoons freshly ground black pepper

½ teaspoon ground allspice

4 to 5 pounds beef oxtails, patted dry

2 tablespoons extra-virgin olive oil,
plus more as needed

3 leeks (white and light green parts),
halved lengthwise and thinly sliced

2 fennel bulbs, trimmed, halved,
and thinly sliced (save the fronds and
chop them for garnish)

2 carrots, cut into ½-inch-thick rounds

1 tablespoon tomato paste

6 large garlic cloves, finely chopped

1 bottle (750 ml) dry red wine

5 sprigs fresh parsley, plus ¼ cup
chopped leaves

2 sprigs fresh rosemary

2 bay leaves

Grated zest of 1 lemon

Oxtails make for a particularly succulent stew because the bones release rich, brawny-flavored marrow while they cook. Here the oxtails are prepared with fennel, carrots, and herbs, which add depth, while a garnish of lemon zest and chopped parsley brightens everything just before serving. I like to serve oxtails still on the bones, since I really love gnawing off the meat. But it is messy, so make sure to have plenty of napkins on hand. Or for something more elegant, make the stew ahead and pull the meat off the bones before serving. That will make it much fork-friendlier. Serve it with something to soak up all the good sauce, like Garlic Rice (page 85), mashed potatoes (see page 135), or crusty bread.

Note that oxtails are generally sold already sliced cross-wise into 1- to 2-inch pieces. The thickness doesn't really matter in terms of cooking, so buy whatever is available. However, if your butcher will cut the oxtails to order, ask for 1-inch slices, which are easier to pick up and eat than larger chunks.

----

1. In a small bowl, combine the salt, pepper, and allspice. Rub the mixture all over the oxtails. Place them in a large bowl and cover with plastic wrap. Refrigerate for at least 1 hour or overnight.

2. Using the sauté function, heat the oil in the pressure cooker (or do this in a skillet over high heat). Add as many oxtails as you can fit in a single layer without overcrowding. Sear, turning them occasionally, until the meat is uniformly golden brown all over, including the sides, 3 to 5 minutes per side. Transfer the meat to a plate; repeat until you've browned all of the oxtails.

3. Add the leeks, fennel, and a pinch of salt to the drippings in the pressure cooker (or skillet), and cook over medium heat until the vegetables are lightly caramelized, about 10 minutes. If the pot or pan looks dry, add a little more oil. Add the carrots and cook until golden, about 5 minutes. Stir in the tomato paste and two-thirds of the garlic (save the rest for the garnish), and cook for 1 minute.

4. Pour the wine into the pot (or skillet). Tie the parsley, rosemary, and bay leaves together with kitchen twine and drop the bundle into the wine. Bring the mixture to a simmer and cook over medium heat until the liquid has reduced by half, about 15 minutes. (If you used a skillet, scrape the mixture into the pressure cooker.) Add the oxtails to the pressure cooker, cover, and cook on high pressure for 45 minutes. Let the pressure release naturally.

5. Transfer the oxtails to a plate. Simmer the sauce on the sauté function until it thickens slightly, 5 to 7 minutes. Oxtails release a lot of fat. If you like, you can use a fat separator to degrease the sauce, or let it settle and spoon off the fat from the top. Discard the herb bundle.

6. Toss the oxtails with some of the sauce. Taste, and adjust the seasonings if necessary. In a small bowl, toss together the chopped parsley, remaining garlic, lemon zest, and a pinch of salt. Scatter the mixture over the oxtails and then garnish with the fennel fronds before serving.

COOK IT SLOW

Nestle the oxtails in among the vegetables, making sure the meat is mostly covered. Cook on high for 7 to 8 hours or low for 10 to 12 hours.

OSSO BUCO

TIME: 2½ HOURS

YIELD: 4 TO 6 SERVINGS

FOR THE OSSO BUCO

All-purpose flour, for dredging

4 sprigs fresh thyme

2 sprigs fresh rosemary

1 bay leaf

2½ to 3 pounds (4 pieces) osso buco
(bone-in veal shanks),
patted dry with a paper towel

2 teaspoons kosher salt

Freshly ground black pepper

3 tablespoons extra-virgin olive oil

2 tablespoons unsalted butter

1 onion, diced into ¼-inch pieces

2 medium carrots, diced into
¼-inch pieces

1 celery stalk, diced into ¼-inch pieces

4 garlic cloves, thinly sliced

½ teaspoon tomato paste

½ cup dry white wine

½ cup chicken or beef stock,
preferably homemade (page 114)

1 14.5-ounce can diced tomatoes,
drained

FOR THE GREMOLATA

¼ cup finely chopped fresh parsley

Finely grated zest of ½ lemon

2 garlic cloves, minced

Pinch of kosher salt, plus more as needed

This classic dish of veal shanks braised in wine and tomatoes is a masterpiece of northern Italian cooking. Be sure to provide small spoons (espresso spoons work well) so people can scoop the marrow out of the bones, then eat the marrow sprinkled with salt and some of the gremolata. Saffron risotto (page 91) is the ideal accompaniment.

---

1. Spread flour in a shallow bowl or plate. Tie the thyme sprigs, rosemary sprigs, and bay leaf together with kitchen twine.

2. Season the veal with the salt and pepper to taste, and then dredge it in the flour to coat all sides. Using the sauté function on high if available, heat the oil in the pressure cooker. Add the osso buco in batches (do not crowd the pot), and brown it well on all sides, 5 to 7 minutes per side. Altogether this will take 20 to 30 minutes to get the pieces nicely golden all over. Transfer the osso buco pieces to a plate as they brown.

3. Turn the sauté function down to medium if available, or unplug the pot for a minute to let it cool down slightly. Add the butter to the pressure cooker and let it melt; then stir in the onion, carrots, and celery. Cook until the vegetables are very soft, about 8 minutes. Stir in the garlic and tomato paste, and cook until the garlic is fragrant and the tomato paste has darkened, another 1 to 2 minutes.

4. Add the wine to the pot to deglaze it, scraping up any browned bits from the bottom. Stir in the stock and tomatoes and bring to a simmer. Nestle the osso buco pieces into the pot, then top with the herb bundle. Cover and cook on high pressure for 40 minutes. Let the pressure release naturally.

5. Transfer the osso buco to a plate and, using the sauté function, simmer the sauce, stirring it often, until it is thick and reduced, 10 to 15 minutes. Let the sauce settle for at least 10 minutes, and then spoon any excess fat off the top.

6. While the sauce is settling, make the gremolata: In a small bowl, stir together the parsley, lemon zest, garlic, and salt.

7. To serve, transfer the osso buco to a serving platter, spoon the sauce over the top, and sprinkle with the gremolata, with more on the side.

COOK IT SLOW

Cook on high for 5 to 7 hours or
on low for 8 to 10 hours.

CLASSIC BOEUF
BOURGUIGNON

TIME: 1½ HOURS

YIELD: 4 TO 6 SERVINGS

————————

3 pounds boneless beef chuck, cut into
2-inch cubes and patted dry

2¼ teaspoons kosher salt,
plus more as needed

½ teaspoon freshly ground black pepper,
plus more as needed

3 ounces pancetta or bacon, diced

1 onion, finely chopped

1 large carrot, cut into ¼-inch-thick coins
(about 1¼ cups)

2 tablespoons all-purpose flour

2 garlic cloves, minced

1 teaspoon tomato paste

2 cups dry red wine

1 large bay leaf

1 large sprig fresh thyme

8 ounces pearl onions (about 2¾ cups)

1 tablespoon unsalted butter

Pinch of sugar

8 ounces cremini mushrooms,
halved if large (about 3½ cups)

Chopped fresh parsley, for serving

————————

A hearty French standard of meat braised in plenty of red wine, beef bourguignon is one of those recipes that will never go out of style. There are many versions of this recipe—as many as there are cooks in Burgundy, it's often said. This one uses bacon and a little tomato paste for depth of flavor. You might notice that the recipe also calls for about half the usual amount of wine. That's because in a pressure cooker, no steam escapes while the meat cooks, so you don't need to use as much liquid. This means you get to sip the wine that's left over in the bottle with your meal, making it more important than ever to choose a wine that's good enough to drink—and it really does make a difference in the finished stew. Serve this with Butter-Braised Yukon Gold Potatoes (page 139), noodles, or rice (see page 84).

————————

1. Season the beef with 2 teaspoons of the salt and the pepper, and let it rest while you sauté the pancetta.

2. Using the sauté function, cook the pancetta in the pressure cooker until the fat is rendered and the pancetta is browned and crispy, 7 to 12 minutes. Transfer with a slotted spoon to a paper-towel-lined plate. Reserve the fat in the pressure cooker. (Or you can do this in a large skillet if you prefer.)

3. Increase the heat to high, if available. Arrange a batch of the beef cubes in a single layer in the pressure cooker (or skillet), leaving space between the pieces. Cook until well browned on all sides, 8 to 12 minutes, transferring them to a plate as they brown. Repeat with the remaining beef.

4. Stir the onion and carrot into the pressure cooker (or skillet), and cook until they start to soften, about 5 minutes. Stir in the flour, garlic, tomato paste, and remaining ¼ teaspoon salt, and cook until fragrant, about 2 minutes. Then stir in the wine, bay leaf, and thyme sprig, scraping up the browned bits on the bottom of the pot. Add the browned beef and half of the cooked pancetta to the pressure cooker (or transfer everything to the cooker if you've used a skillet). Cover and cook on high pressure for 20 minutes. Allow the pressure to release naturally.

5. Open the lid, turn on the sauté function, and cook until the sauce is thick, 7 to 12 minutes.

6. Meanwhile, cook the pearl onions and mushrooms: In a large skillet set over high heat, combine the pearl onions, butter, and a pinch each of salt, pepper, and sugar. Bring to a simmer, and then cover and reduce the heat to medium; cook until the onions turn golden brown, 15 minutes. Uncover, add the mushrooms, raise heat to high, and cook, tossing frequently, until all the vegetables are well browned, 5 to 7 minutes.

7. To serve, scatter the onions and mushrooms and remaining cooked pancetta over the stew, then top it with the parsley.

COOK IT SLOW

Cook on high for 5 to 7 hours or low for 8 to 10 hours.

LAMB TAGINE
WITH APRICOTS
+ OLIVES

TIME: 1 HOUR 15 MINUTES,
PLUS AT LEAST 1 HOUR MARINATING
YIELD: 4 TO 6 SERVINGS

———————

3 pounds bone-in lamb stew meat or lamb neck, fat trimmed, cut into 2-inch chunks

2¼ teaspoons kosher salt, plus more as needed

2 tablespoons extra-virgin olive oil, plus more as needed

2 large onions, thinly sliced

1 teaspoon tomato paste

1 teaspoon grated peeled fresh ginger

1 small cinnamon stick

½ teaspoon ground ginger

¾ teaspoon ground turmeric

¾ teaspoon finely ground black pepper

¼ teaspoon ground cinnamon

Pinch of freshly grated nutmeg

1½ cups lamb or chicken stock, preferably homemade (page 114)

5 ounces (1 cup) dried apricots, halved or quartered if large

¼ cup coarsely chopped fresh cilantro, plus more for serving

Large pinch of saffron threads

A fragrant mix of spices including ginger, cinnamon, nutmeg, and saffron gives this North African stew its robust character and seductive aroma, which will perfume your whole kitchen once you take the top off the pot. Serve it with flatbread or couscous to soak up the juices. You won't want to leave any behind.

———————

1. In a large bowl, combine the lamb and 2 teaspoons of the salt. Let sit for at least 1 hour or up to 24 hours in the fridge.

2. Turn the pressure cooker to the sauté function (or heat a skillet over medium-high heat). Add 1 tablespoon of the oil and heat until hot. Add the lamb pieces in batches, leaving room around each piece (this will help them brown), and cook until well browned on all sides, about 12 minutes. If the pan looks dry, add a bit more oil as you go. Transfer each piece of the lamb to a bowl once it browns.

3. Add another tablespoon of the oil to the pressure cooker (or skillet), and let it heat for a few seconds. Then add the onions and remaining ¼ teaspoon salt and cook until the onions are soft, 8 to 10 minutes. Add the tomato paste, fresh ginger, 1 cinnamon stick, and the ground ginger, turmeric, pepper, cinnamon, and nutmeg. Cook until fragrant, about 2 minutes.

4. If you used a skillet, transfer the mixture to the pressure cooker. Add the lamb and any juices in the bowl, along with the stock, apricots, cilantro, and saffron. Cover and cook on high pressure for 25 minutes. Let the pressure release naturally.

5. Meanwhile, in a small skillet, heat the butter and cinnamon stick over medium heat. Add the almonds and a pinch of salt; cook until the almonds are golden brown, 5 to 7 minutes. Discard the cinnamon stick.

6. Using a slotted spoon, transfer the lamb to a large bowl. Turn on the sauté function and simmer the sauce until it is thickened to taste, 5 to 10 minutes; adjust the seasonings if necessary. Stir in the lamb, and the olives if using.

7. To serve, transfer the lamb and sauce to a serving platter. Top with the toasted almonds and any butter in the skillet, along with the olives (if using), scallions, parsley, and more cilantro. Sprinkle with lemon juice to taste.

FOR SERVING

1 tablespoon unsalted butter

½ cup slivered blanched almonds

⅓ cup sliced pitted green olives (optional)

2 scallions (white and green parts), finely chopped

2 tablespoons chopped fresh parsley

Fresh lemon juice, to taste

COOK IT SLOW

Cook on high for 7 to 9 hours or low for 10 to 12 hours.

BRAISED ROMAN-STYLE LAMB
WITH HERBS + PEAS

**TIME: 2 HOURS,
PLUS AT LEAST 1 HOUR MARINATING
YIELD: 6 SERVINGS
GF**

**3½ pounds boneless lamb shoulder,
well trimmed, cut into 2 pieces**

**9 garlic cloves: 3 finely grated,
6 left whole**

**2 teaspoons kosher salt,
plus more as needed**

½ teaspoon freshly ground black pepper

**6 sprigs fresh thyme
(lemon thyme is particularly nice here),
torn or cut into pieces**

**4 sprigs fresh rosemary,
torn or cut into pieces**

2 tablespoons extra-virgin olive oil

**2 leeks (white and light green parts only),
or 1 large onion, diced**

1 cup dry white wine

6 oil-packed anchovy fillets

Pinch of crushed red pepper flakes

Fresh lemon juice, to taste

**1 cup shelled peas, fresh or frozen
(do not thaw)**

1 tablespoon chopped fresh tarragon

**2 scallions (white and green parts),
thinly sliced**

**Chopped fresh mint and/or more tarragon,
for serving**

Perfect for springtime, this ethereally tender lamb has an intense, heady sauce flecked with herbs and sweet green peas. The anchovies add a saline complexity but aren't at all fishy. Plus, no one will know they are there if you don't tell them. Serve this with something—bread, rice, polenta, or a spoon—to scoop up the sauce. It's quite spectacular and you won't want to miss a drop.

---

1. In a large bowl, toss the lamb with the grated garlic, salt, pepper, and thyme and rosemary sprigs. Cover and refrigerate for at least 1 hour, and preferably overnight.

2. Brush the herbs off the lamb and reserve. Using the sauté function in the pressure cooker (or a skillet over high heat), heat 1 tablespoon of the oil. Once it is hot, add the lamb. Let it brown for 5 to 7 minutes per side, and then transfer the pieces to a plate.

3. Add another tablespoon of the oil to the pot (or skillet). When it's hot, add the leeks and sauté until golden, 3 to 5 minutes (if the pot gets too hot and you can't lower the heat, turn it off for a few minutes and let the leeks cook in the residual heat to keep them from burning).

4. Add the wine to the pot (or skillet) and simmer, scraping up the browned bits, until it has reduced by half, about 2 minutes. Add the anchovies and red pepper flakes. Return the lamb and reserved herb sprigs to the pot, cover, and cook on high pressure for 50 minutes. Let the pressure release naturally.

5. Using a slotted spoon, transfer the lamb to a serving platter. Use a fat separator to separate the fat from the juices, or just spoon the fat off the top. Taste the sauce, and add more salt and/or a squeeze of lemon as needed. If the sauce is thin, use the sauté function to simmer it down.

6. Stir in the peas and tarragon and simmer on the sauté function until peas are tender (1 to 2 minutes for frozen peas, 2 to 5 for fresh peas). Serve the lamb topped with scallions and mint, and a squeeze of lemon juice if desired.

COOK IT SLOW

—

Cook the lamb on high for 5 to 7 hours
or low for 8 to 10 hours, adding the
peas during the last 5 minutes.

BRAISED PORK
WITH GARLIC, FENNEL + OLIVES

TIME: 1 HOUR 15 MINUTES,
PLUS AT LEAST 1 HOUR MARINATING
YIELD: 4 TO 6 SERVINGS

GF

**4 pounds boneless pork shoulder,
cut into 2-inch pieces**

**1 tablespoon kosher salt,
plus more as needed**

**4 garlic cloves, grated on a Microplane
or minced**

**¼ cup chopped fresh basil,
plus more for serving**

1 tablespoon chopped fresh rosemary

1 teaspoon chopped fresh sage

1 teaspoon finely grated lemon zest

½ teaspoon freshly ground black pepper

½ teaspoon crushed red pepper flakes

1 teaspoon fennel seeds

**2 tablespoons olive oil,
plus more as needed**

⅔ cup dry white wine

Squeeze of fresh lemon juice (optional)

½ cup good pitted green olives, sliced

Shaved Parmesan cheese, for serving

COOK IT SLOW

Cook the pork on high for 6 to 8 hours
or low for 10 to 12 hours.

Inspired by the flavors of an Italian porchetta, this soft and rich braised pork has plenty of herbs, lemon, and fennel to balance out the red pepper flakes and garlic. If you can plan ahead, make this the day before you want to serve it. The flavors will meld, making it even more delicious. The fat will also be easier to remove after chilling—you'll be able to spoon the solid layer right off before reheating the dish.

Serve it over polenta (page 93) or rice (page 84) to absorb all the heady juices.

---

1. In a large bowl, combine the pork, salt, garlic, basil, rosemary, sage, lemon zest, black pepper, and red pepper flakes.

2. In a small dry skillet over medium heat, toast the fennel seeds until fragrant, 1 to 2 minutes. Transfer to a mortar and pestle and crush lightly (or do this on a cutting board with the side of a heavy knife). Add to pork and toss. Cover and refrigerate for 1 hour or overnight.

3. Using the sauté function (or do this in a skillet), add 1 tablespoon of the oil to the pressure cooker and let it get hot for a few seconds; then add enough pork cubes to fit comfortably in one layer with a little space around each piece. Let them brown for 2 to 3 minutes per side, and then transfer them to a plate. Add a little more oil if the pot looks dry, and continue browning the rest of the pork.

4. Add the wine and let it simmer, scraping up the browned bits, until it has reduced by half, about 2 minutes. Return pork to the pot, cover, and cook on high pressure for 1 hour. Allow the pressure to release naturally.

5. Using a slotted spoon, transfer the pork to a serving platter and tent with foil to keep warm. Use a fat separator to separate the fat from the juices, or just spoon the fat off the top (there will be a lot of it). If the sauce seems thin, use the sauté function to simmer it until it thickens to taste. Taste the sauce, and add more salt and/or a squeeze of lemon to taste. Stir the olives into the sauce, remove the foil from the platter, and pour the sauce over the meat. Serve the pork topped with more basil and some shaved Parmesan cheese.

SMOKY BARBECUE CHICKEN

TIME: 1 HOUR

YIELD: 4 TO 6 SERVINGS

___

FOR THE CHICKEN

2½ pounds boneless, skinless chicken thighs

1 teaspoon kosher salt

FOR THE BARBECUE SAUCE

½ cup ketchup

1 tablespoon packed dark brown sugar

2 teaspoons molasses

2 teaspoons Worcestershire sauce

2 teaspoons chopped chipotle chile in adobo sauce (optional)

1 teaspoon apple cider vinegar

1 garlic clove, grated on a Microplane or minced

¾ teaspoon sweet or hot smoked paprika

½ teaspoon freshly ground black pepper

¼ teaspoon dry mustard powder

FOR SERVING

Hot sauce, to taste (optional)

___

Zesty, just a little spicy, and very flavorful, this chicken is just as pleasing rolled into tortillas or made into sandwiches as it is served over rice or with mac and cheese.

If you like, you can substitute ½ cup of your favorite barbecue sauce here instead of making your own. Just make sure to cook it down to a paste in step 2 before adding the chicken to the pot; otherwise you might be left with too much liquid at the end.

___

1. Season the chicken thighs with the salt and let them sit while you prepare the sauce.

2. For the barbecue sauce, set the pressure cooker on the sauté function. Add the ketchup, brown sugar, molasses, Worcestershire, chipotle chile, vinegar, and garlic. Stir in the paprika, black pepper, and dry mustard, and simmer until the mixture is darkened and thick (it should turn into a paste), 3 to 5 minutes.

3. Stir in the chicken. Cover and cook on high pressure for 15 minutes. Let the pressure release naturally.

4. Using tongs, transfer the chicken to a large bowl, leaving the sauce in the pressure cooker. Set the cooker on the sauté function and simmer the sauce until it has thickened to taste (remembering that it will continue to thicken as it cools), 5 to 10 minutes. Meanwhile, shred the chicken. Toss the chicken with some of the barbecue sauce and season with hot sauce to taste. Serve the remaining sauce on the side.

COOK IT SLOW

___

Cook the sauce slightly less—it should bubble for a minute but not turn into a paste. Stir in the chicken, making sure it is well coated in the sauce. Cook on high for 3 to 4 hours or low for 4 to 5 hours.

CHICKEN + DUMPLINGS

TIME: 1 HOUR 30 MINUTES,
PLUS 20 MINUTES MARINATING
YIELD: 4 SERVINGS

FOR THE CHICKEN

3½ pounds bone-in chicken pieces, preferably dark meat

1½ teaspoons kosher salt, plus more as needed

½ teaspoon freshly ground black pepper

4 tablespoons (½ stick) unsalted butter

2 carrots, diced

2 celery stalks, diced

1 Spanish onion, diced

1 turnip, peeled and diced

4 garlic cloves, smashed

¼ cup all-purpose flour

1 quart chicken stock, preferably homemade (page 114)

Chopped fresh parsley or celery leaves, for serving

FOR THE DUMPLINGS

1½ cups all-purpose flour

½ cup fine cornmeal

¼ cup minced fresh chive (optional)

2 teaspoons baking powder

¾ teaspoon kosher salt

¼ teaspoon freshly ground black pepper

2 tablespoons butter, melted

¾ cup whole milk

It doesn't get more comforting than a simmering pot of chicken and soft, fluffy dumplings. This one is relatively classic, though I've added some chives to the dumplings for color and freshness. But feel free to leave them out for something more traditionally beige. Or stir in a handful of thawed frozen peas at the end for sweetness and a touch of green.

I prefer using all dark meat here—a combination of drumsticks and thighs gives great flavor and won't over-cook as readily as white meat. But use whatever pieces you like, or a combination. If using all white meat, cook it for a minute or two less.

---

1. In a large bowl, toss the chicken pieces with the salt and pepper. Let them sit for 20 minutes.

2. Using the sauté function, melt 2 tablespoons of the butter in the pressure cooker. Add the chicken pieces, in batches, and brown them on all sides until deep golden brown, about 5 minutes per side. Transfer the chicken to a plate.

3. Add the remaining 2 tablespoons butter to the pressure cooker and stir in the carrots, celery, onion, turnip, and garlic cloves. Cook until softened, about 10 minutes. Then stir in the flour and cook until the mixture starts to turn golden, about another 3 minutes. Stir in the chicken stock, scraping up the browned bits from the bottom of the pot, and nestle the browned chicken into the vegetables. Cover and cook on high pressure for 13 minutes, and then release the pressure manually. Transfer the chicken pieces to a plate, reserving the broth in the pot. When the chicken is cool enough to handle, remove the bones and skin if you like, and tear the meat into chunks.

4. Meanwhile, make the dumplings: In a medium bowl, whisk together the flour, cornmeal, chives if using, baking powder, salt, and pepper. Pour the melted butter and the milk into the flour mixture, and stir gently with a spoon or spatula until just combined. Drop spoonfuls of the batter into the broth in the pot, spacing them evenly across the surface. Cover and cook on high pressure for 10 minutes.

Let the pressure release naturally for 15 minutes, and then release the remaining pressure manually.

5. Test the dumplings by cutting into one and making sure it's cooked all the way through. If not, turn the sauté function on and simmer the dumplings until they are done.

6. Stir the chicken back into the pot to warm it up, and serve it topped with parsley or celery leaves.

COOK IT SLOW

Add the stock plus ½ cup water, bring to a simmer, and cook on high until the chicken is tender, 3 to 4 hours. Transfer the chicken to a plate. Drop spoonfuls of the batter into the slow cooker, cover, and cook on high until cooked through, 1½ to 2 hours, depending upon size.

COQ AU VIN ROSÉ

TIME: 1 HOUR 45 MINUTES

YIELD: 4 TO 6 SERVINGS

————————

3 to 4 pounds skin-on whole chicken legs (drumsticks and thighs)

2¼ teaspoons kosher salt, plus more to taste

½ teaspoon freshly ground black pepper, plus more to taste

2½ cups dry rosé wine

1 bay leaf

1 teaspoon fresh thyme leaves

Extra-virgin olive oil, as needed

3 ounces pancetta or bacon, diced into ¼-inch pieces (about ¾ cup)

3 large shallots, diced

1 large carrot, diced

8 ounces cremini or white button mushrooms, halved if large, sliced (about 4 cups)

2 garlic cloves, grated on a Microplane or minced

1½ tablespoons all-purpose flour

1 tablespoon brandy

1 tablespoon unsalted butter

8 ounces (12 to 15) pearl onions

Pinch of sugar

Chopped fresh parsley, for serving

————————

Most coq au vin recipes call for red wine, giving you something deeply hearty and richly purple. This one, using rosé wine, is a lighter, brighter, and more delicate take that lets the flavors of the mushrooms, pancetta, and herbs shine. However, if you'd prefer something more classic, simply use red wine instead.

In either case, you'll have about a cup of wine left over after opening the bottle. That's for you, the cook, to enjoy while the chicken is cooking.

————————

1. Season the chicken legs with 2 teaspoons of the salt and the pepper. In a large bowl, combine the chicken, wine, bay leaf, and thyme. Cover and let it sit while you prepare the pancetta.

2. Using the sauté function, drizzle a little oil in the pressure cooker and spread the pancetta in an even layer. Cook, stirring often, until the fat has rendered and the meat is golden and crispy, 5 to 7 minutes. Using a slotted spoon, transfer the pancetta to a paper-towel-lined plate, leaving the rendered fat in the pot.

3. Remove the chicken legs from the wine, reserving the marinade, and pat them dry. Add the chicken to the pot in a single layer (do this in batches if necessary) and cook until it is well browned, 4 to 5 minutes per side. (Add oil if the pot looks a little dry.) Transfer the chicken legs to a plate as they brown.

4. Add the shallots, carrot, half of the mushrooms, and the remaining ¼ teaspoon salt to the pot and cook, stirring up any browned bits, until the vegetables are lightly browned, about 5 minutes.

5. Stir in the garlic and cook for 1 minute; then stir in the flour and cook for another minute. Add the brandy and the reserved marinade, bring to a boil, and cook until the liquid has reduced by half (to 1½ cups), about 12 minutes. Skim off any large pockets of foam that form on the surface.

6. Add the chicken, any accumulated juices, and half of the cooked pancetta to the pot, cover it, and cook on high pressure for 13 minutes. Then release the pressure manually.

7. Meanwhile, melt the butter and 2 tablespoons olive oil in a large skillet (nonstick is preferable) over medium-high heat. Add the pearl onions, sugar, and salt to taste, cover the skillet, reduce the heat to low, and cook for 15 minutes, shaking the skillet often to move the onions around. Uncover, push the onions to one side of the skillet, add the remaining mushrooms, and raise the heat to medium-high. Cook, uncovered, stirring the mushrooms frequently and gently tossing the onions occasionally, until everything is browned, 5 to 8 minutes.

8. When the chicken is done, use a slotted spoon to transfer it to a platter and set it aside. Using the sauté function, simmer the liquid in the pressure cooker until the sauce thickens to the desired texture, 8 to 10 minutes. Taste, and add salt and pepper if necessary.

9. To serve, return the chicken to the pressure cooker to reheat it in the sauce, adding the pearl onions, mushrooms, and remaining half of the cooked pancetta. Baste with the wine sauce, sprinkle with parsley, and serve.

COOK IT SLOW

Cook on high for 5 to 7 hours or low for 7 to 9 hours.

COCONUT CURRY
CHICKEN

TIME: 1 HOUR

YIELD: 4 SERVINGS

GF

---

3 to 4 ripe tomatoes,
halved through their equators

3 tablespoons ghee, unsalted butter,
or safflower oil

3 tablespoons virgin coconut oil

2 cups finely chopped onions

6 garlic cloves, grated on a Microplane
or minced

2 tablespoons grated peeled fresh ginger

1 teaspoon cumin seeds

1 3-inch cinnamon stick or ½ teaspoon
ground cinnamon

8 cardamom pods, lightly crushed with
the flat side of a knife, or 1 teaspoon
ground cardamom

2 teaspoons ground coriander

1 tablespoon kosher salt

1 teaspoon ground turmeric

¼ teaspoon crushed red pepper flakes

¼ teaspoon freshly ground black pepper

2½ pounds boneless, skinless chicken
thighs, cut into 1-inch chunks

1 to 2 teaspoons garam masala, to taste

½ cup canned unsweetened coconut milk

Cooked basmati rice, for serving

3 tablespoons finely chopped
fresh cilantro

Plain yogurt, for serving (optional)

Dried coconut (strips or shredded),
for serving

The highly spiced coconut sauce here is so good, you'll want to slather it on anything!

And it's a great and adaptable medium for cooking other proteins—not just chicken. Try cubes of lamb, fish fillets, or chunks of pork. Or, if you prefer boneless chicken breasts to thighs, use them here, pressure-cooking them for 2 minutes instead of 4.

When serving, tell your guests to be aware of the cardamom pods so they don't accidentally bite into one—or use the ground cardamom instead. And note that brands of garam masala vary in terms of their chile content, so some are hotter than others. If you're unsure how hot your mix is, add it gradually to the pot, tasting as you go.

---

1. Set a box grater over a bowl. Starting with their cut sides, grate the tomatoes through the large holes of the box grater so the tomato pulp falls into the bowl. Discard the skins. Measure out 2 cups of tomato puree.

2. Using the sauté function, heat the ghee and the coconut oil in the pressure cooker. Stir in the onions and cook, stirring often to encourage even browning, until they are caramelized, 12 to 18 minutes. Stir in the garlic, ginger, and cumin seeds; cook until fragrant, about 2 minutes. Stir in the cinnamon and cardamom and cook for another minute. Then stir in the coriander, salt, turmeric, red pepper flakes, black pepper, and finally the tomato puree.

3. Add the chicken to the sauce, cover, and cook on low pressure for 4 minutes. Let the pressure release naturally. If the sauce seems too thin, use a slotted spoon to transfer the chicken to a bowl and then simmer the sauce on the sauté setting until it has thickened to taste (note that the coconut milk, if you are using it, will thin the sauce down further). Stir in the garam masala, and the coconut milk if using, and let the curry sit for 20 minutes for the flavors to meld. Serve over rice, topped with the cilantro and yogurt, if desired.

COOK IT SLOW

Cook on high for 2 to 3 hours or low for 4 to 5 hours, adding the coconut milk, if using, during the last hour.

MIDDLE EASTERN
SPICED
CHICKEN
+ RICE WITH EGGPLANT

TIME: 2 HOURS

YIELD: 8 TO 10 SERVINGS

GF

———

1½ pounds boneless, skinless chicken thighs

1½ teaspoons baharat spice blend (see Note)

1 tablespoon plus 1½ teaspoons kosher salt, plus more as needed

1¼ teaspoons freshly ground black pepper

3 cups basmati rice

1 large or 2 small eggplants (1¼ pounds total), halved lengthwise and cut into 1-inch-thick half-moons

1 medium zucchini, sliced into ½-inch-thick rounds

1 large Spanish onion, halved from root to stem and sliced into half-moons

1 red bell pepper, seeded and sliced into ¼-inch-thick strips

4 tablespoons extra-virgin olive oil, plus more as needed

6 sprigs fresh thyme

1 teaspoon ground turmeric

1 teaspoon ground cumin

1 teaspoon ground cinnamon

½ teaspoon ground cardamom

Chopped fresh mint or cilantro

Whole-milk yogurt, for serving (optional)

———

Fragrant with cinnamon, cumin, and cardamom and layered with tender chicken and velvety slices of roasted eggplant, this Middle Eastern rice dish called Maqluba, is one of the more elaborate and exciting things to make in an electric pressure cooker. It does take some advance prep work: the chicken needs to get marinated, the rice needs to soak, and the vegetables need to roast until caramelized all over. But it's well worth the effort for the bronzed, crisp-edged dish that emerges in a cloud of aromatic steam. Serve this for a dinner party, with something piquant on the side (chopped preserved lemons, some kind of spicy chutney, or even your favorite salsa). All that lovely rice benefits from a kick.

You can use skinless, boneless, chicken breast halves here if you prefer, but the thighs stay juicier. And if you have a nonstick insert for your pressure cooker, consider using it here. It will be easier to unmold at the end.

———

1. Heat the oven to 425°F.

2. In a medium bowl, combine the chicken, ½ teaspoon of the baharat, 1 teaspoon of the salt, and ¼ teaspoon of the pepper. Let it sit while you work on everything else.

3. In a separate bowl, rinse the rice several times until the water runs clear; then cover the rice with warm water and let it soak while the vegetables roast.

4. Put the eggplant on one rimmed baking sheet and the zucchini on another; then combine the onion and bell pepper on a third rimmed baking sheet. Toss the vegetables with the olive oil (about 1 tablespoon per sheet) and season with salt to taste. Top each baking sheet with 2 thyme sprigs. Roast until the vegetables are browned at the edges, flipping them over halfway through: 40 minutes for the eggplant and zucchini, 30 minutes for the onions and peppers. Remove the thyme sprigs and set the baking sheets aside.

5. Drain the rice and mix in the remaining 1 teaspoon baharat along with the turmeric, cumin, cinnamon, cardamom, and the remaining 1 tablespoon plus ½ teaspoon salt.

6. Using the sauté function, heat the remaining 1 tablespoon oil in the pressure cooker, making sure to swirl it to coat the bottom evenly. Place half of the chicken in an even layer in the pot, and then scatter one-third of the rice around the chicken, patting it down loosely to form an even layer. Lay the onions and peppers on top in an even layer, and sprinkle them lightly with a scoopful of rice. Then layer the eggplant and zucchini, and sprinkle them with another scoop of rice (to total about another one-third of the rice). Place the remaining chicken on top, and then gently pat the remaining rice around it.

7. Pour 4 cups of water down the edges of the pot, cover, and cook on high pressure for 4 minutes. Release the pressure manually.

8. Uncover the pot, drape a clean dish towel over the top, and then place the cover (or use a plate) back on the pot and let it sit for 10 minutes.

9. To serve, you have two choices: You can scoop the maqluba out onto a serving platter. Or for the brave, you can unmold it onto a platter: Remove the pressure cooker pot (using oven mitts or kitchen towels—the pot will be hot) and run a long offset spatula around the edge of the pot to loosen the rice. Invert a large platter on top of the pot, and then quickly flip them over together so the rice falls in a large mound onto the platter (using a nonstick insert makes this easier). It may or may not come out in one piece (as a giant cake), but it will be delicious even if it falls apart. Garnish the rice with mint and yogurt, and serve.

NOTE: BAHARAT is a Middle Eastern spice mix. You can buy it at specialty markets, or you can easily make your own by combining:

> 2 tablespoons sweet paprika
> 1 tablespoon ground coriander
> 1 tablespoon ground cumin
> 1 tablespoon ground turmeric
> 2 teaspoons freshly ground black pepper
> 1 teaspoon grated nutmeg
> 1 teaspoon ground cardamom
> 1 teaspoon allspice

YIELD: ½ cup. (It will last for up to 6 months when stored in an airtight jar at room temperature.)

DUCK CONFIT

TIME: 2 HOURS,
PLUS AT LEAST 24 HOURS CURING

YIELD: 4 SERVINGS

GF • P

1 tablespoon kosher salt

4 sprigs fresh thyme

4 garlic cloves, smashed

2 bay leaves, torn in half

¼ teaspoon black peppercorns,
lightly crushed

¼ teaspoon allspice berries,
lightly crushed

4 duck legs (drumsticks and thighs)

NOTE: This recipe requires you to cure (marinate) the duck legs in salt, spices, garlic, and herbs at least a day or two ahead of cooking. This is an essential part of making duck confit. The salt draws out some of the moisture from the duck, firming up its texture, and the aromatics infuse it with flavor.

Serve the duck confit on its own as an entrée, perhaps with the Garlicky Beans with Broccoli Rabe (page 111) on the side. Or plop it on a bed of bitter greens for a rich and luxurious salad.

This recipe might be my favorite way to use the electric pressure cooker: it is an easy and relatively quick method for making meltingly tender duck confit. You won't need to add any extra duck fat to the pot; the duck here cooks in its own rendered fat, after which it emerges soft-fleshed and flavorful, and ready to be quickly crisped up under the broiler before serving. You'll also end up with extra rendered duck fat. I like to save that fat for frying and roasting. Store it in an airtight container in the refrigerator, where it will last for up to 3 months, or freeze it for up to a year. It is absolutely wonderful for cooking potatoes.

1. Line a small rimmed baking sheet or a plate with paper towels. In a large bowl, stir together the salt, thyme, garlic, bay leaves, peppercorns, and allspice. Add the duck legs and toss, covering the legs evenly with the salt. Place the duck legs in a single layer on the baking sheet and refrigerate, uncovered, for at least 24 hours and up to 3 days.

2. Brush the garlic and thyme sprigs off the duck, reserving them. Using the sauté function, arrange the duck legs, skin-side down, in the pressure cooker, with as much of the flesh touching the bottom of the pot as possible. Sear until the skin turns golden brown and the fat starts to render, 5 to 10 minutes. Flip the duck legs over and sear on the other side for 5 to 10 minutes. Scatter the reserved garlic and thyme on top of the duck.

3. Cover and cook the duck legs on high pressure for 40 minutes, and then release the pressure manually. Flip the legs over, and cook on high pressure for another 30 minutes. Let the pressure release naturally.

4. Let the duck cool completely, and then store it, covered in its own rendered fat (there will be lots of it in the pot), in the refrigerator. Note that you will be left with a dark brown liquid—the duck stock—that will separate from the white duck fat as the confit cools. Save this delicious elixir. You can use it for sauces, soups, or anywhere you need a good, concentrated meat or poultry stock. It also freezes well.

5. When you are ready to serve, heat the broiler.

6. Scrape fat off duck legs. Transfer the duck to a rimmed baking sheet and broil until the skin is crispy, 3 to 5 minutes (or you can crisp up the duck in a hot, dry skillet).

SEAFOOD

SHRIMP SCAMPI
WITH WHITE WINE + FENNEL

TIME: 30 MINUTES

YIELD: 4 SERVINGS

GF (USING GLUTEN-FREE PASTA AND
HOMEMADE CHICKEN STOCK, PAGE 114)

———

2 tablespoons unsalted butter

2 tablespoons extra-virgin olive oil,
plus more as needed

½ cup thinly sliced fennel
(reserve fennel fronds for garnish)

5 garlic cloves, minced

¼ cup dry white wine or fish
or chicken stock

1½ teaspoons kosher salt,
plus more as needed

¼ teaspoon crushed red pepper flakes,
plus more as needed

Freshly ground black pepper to taste

2 pounds extra-large shrimp,
shelled and deveined

8 ounces thin spaghetti, broken in half

Fennel pollen or ground fennel seeds,
for garnish (optional)

½ lemon, for squeezing

———

In this version of shrimp scampi, the shrimp are quickly sautéed in a pungent mix of garlic, wine, chile flakes, and fennel before being removed from the pot. The resulting liquid is then used to cook pasta under pressure, where the noodles can fully absorb its saline, herbal flavor. It's a fast and intense dish that's weeknight friendly but company worthy.

———

1. Using the sauté function, melt the butter and oil in the pressure cooker. Stir in the fennel and garlic, and cook until fragrant, about 2 minutes. Stir in the wine, salt, red pepper flakes, and black pepper, and simmer until the wine has reduced by half, about 1 minute.

2. Stir in the shrimp and cook until they just turn pink but are not fully cooked in the center, about 1 minute. Using a slotted spoon, transfer the shrimp to a large bowl.

3. Carefully pour the liquid from the pot into a large heat-proof measuring cup, and then add enough water to measure 1½ cups. Return the liquid to the pot, stir in the pasta, a generous drizzle of olive oil, and a large pinch of salt, and toss very well to coat the pasta with the sauce and to encourage the strands to separate.

4. Cover and cook on high pressure for 6 minutes. Release the pressure manually. Stir the reserved shrimp and any accumulated juices into the pot, cover, and let sit for 5 minutes for the shrimp to finish cooking.

5. To serve, transfer the pasta and shrimp to a serving platter, and garnish with the reserved fennel fronds, fennel pollen if using, more red pepper flakes, a squeeze of lemon juice to taste, and a generous drizzle of olive oil.

MUSSELS
WITH GARLIC
+ LAGER

TIME: 30 MINUTES

YIELD: 2 SERVINGS

———

2 pounds mussels in shells

1 tablespoon extra-virgin olive oil

3 tablespoons unsalted butter

1 small onion, sliced

Pinch of kosher salt

Freshly ground black pepper to taste

4 garlic cloves, thinly sliced

**⅓ cup mild lager or pilsner beer
(nothing too bitter; avoid IPAs)**

¼ cup chopped fresh parsley

Crusty bread, for serving

———

Most mussels recipes call for steaming the mollusks in a combination of dry white wine and some kind of allium, either garlic or shallots. This one calls for both onion and garlic, but nixes the wine. Instead, mild lager beer lends a toasted, gently bitter flavor that's wonderful with the butter that's mixed in right at the end. Serve this with a baguette or other bread for dunking in the broth, which is arguably just as delicious as the sweet mussels themselves.

Also to note: Most mussels you buy at the fishmonger's have been farmed and are very clean. So there's no need to scrub or soak or de-beard them unless you've harvested them yourself off a rocky, seaweed-laden coast (or are lucky enough to find wild mussels at your fish store). A quick rinse is all the farmed kind need before going into the pot.

———

1. Rinse the mussels under cold running water.

2. Using the sauté function, on low if available, heat the oil and 1 tablespoon of the butter in the pressure cooker. Stir in the onion, salt, and pepper, and sauté until the onion is golden, about 7 minutes. Stir in the garlic and cook until fragrant, another minute. Pour in the beer and bring to a simmer. Add the mussels, cover, and cook on low pressure for 1 minute; then release the pressure manually. Transfer just the mussels, using a slotted spoon, to serving bowls, discarding any that haven't opened.

3. Whisk the parsley and remaining 2 tablespoons butter into the pot; then taste, and adjust the seasoning if necessary. Pour the sauce over the mussels, and serve with bread for sopping up the juices.

INDIAN BUTTER
SHRIMP

TIME: 45 MINUTES,
PLUS 15 TO 60 MINUTES MARINATING
YIELD: 6 SERVINGS
GF

FOR THE MARINADE

¼ cup plain whole-milk yogurt

2 teaspoons ground cumin

2 teaspoons sweet smoked paprika

2 teaspoons garam masala

2 teaspoons fresh lime juice

1½ teaspoons kosher salt

1 teaspoon freshly grated peeled ginger

1 garlic clove, grated on a Microplane
or minced

2 pounds large shrimp,
peeled and deveined

FOR THE SAUCE

4 tablespoons (½ stick) unsalted butter

2 shallots, minced

2 garlic cloves, grated or minced

1½ teaspoons grated peeled fresh ginger

¼ to ½ teaspoon crushed red pepper
flakes, to taste

¼ teaspoon kosher salt,
plus more as needed

1 28-ounce can diced tomatoes
and their juices

1 cup heavy cream

½ teaspoon finely grated lime zest

Cooked basmati rice, for serving

Chopped fresh cilantro, for serving

A play on the classic Indian chicken makhani, in this recipe yogurt and lime juice–marinated shrimp are cooked in a buttery, gently spiced tomato mixture. The key here is to cook the sauce under pressure, but to use the sauté function to quickly cook the shrimp so they don't turn rubbery. Serve this over rice (see page 84) to catch every drop of the fragrant, creamy sauce. If you're a fan of Indian pickles—lime, lemon, mango, and the like—a spoonful of one or all three on the side would not be out of place.

---

1. In a large bowl, mix together the yogurt, cumin, paprika, garam masala, lime juice, salt, ginger, and garlic. Stir in the shrimp, cover the bowl, and refrigerate until needed, at least 15 minutes and up to 1 hour.

2. Prepare the sauce: Using the sauté function, set on low if available, melt 2 tablespoons of the butter in the pressure cooker. Stir in the shallots and a pinch of salt; cook until golden brown, 4 to 8 minutes. Then stir in the garlic, ginger, red pepper flakes, and the ¼ teaspoon salt, and cook until golden, another 1 to 2 minutes.

3. Stir in the tomatoes, cream, and a pinch of salt. Raise the sauté heat to high if available, and bring to a boil. Then cover and cook on high pressure for 8 minutes. Release the pressure manually.

4. Remove the lid, and using the sauté function, simmer the sauce, stirring often, until thickened, 3 to 7 minutes.

5. Stir in the shrimp and the liquid in the bowl, remaining 2 tablespoons butter, and lime zest, and simmer until the shrimp are pink and cooked through, 2 to 5 minutes. Serve over basmati rice, sprinkled with fresh cilantro.

THAI COCONUT CLAMS

TIME: 30 MINUTES

YIELD: 4 TO 6 SERVINGS AS AN APPETIZER,
2 SERVINGS AS AN ENTRÉE

GF (USING VEGETABLE BROTH OR
CHICKEN STOCK, PAGE 114)

---

1 tablespoon coconut oil

3 shallots, halved lengthwise and sliced

1 stalk fresh lemongrass

½ cup vegetable broth or chicken stock,
preferably homemade (page 114)

1 1-inch piece of fresh ginger,
peeled and cut into matchsticks

2 jalapeño peppers, seeded and sliced

2 tablespoons Asian fish sauce

1 tablespoon light brown sugar

½ cup canned full-fat coconut milk
(not refrigerated nondairy beverage)

2 pounds clams, scrubbed

Salt and freshly ground black pepper
to taste

1 scallion (white and green parts),
chopped

½ cup fresh cilantro leaves, chopped

1 lime, cut into wedges, for squeezing

These Thai-inspired clams are salty, tangy, and rich from the coconut milk. If you can't find fresh lemongrass, substitute a couple of sliced garlic cloves and the grated zest from half a lime instead. The broth won't have quite the same flavor, but it will still taste terrific.

---

1. Using the sauté function, heat the oil in the pressure cooker. Add the shallots and sauté until they are soft and browned at the edges, 3 to 5 minutes.

2. Meanwhile, peel the outer layers from the lemongrass stalk and smash the inner core with the side of a heavy knife to bruise it (this helps release the flavor). Finely chop the core.

3. Add the lemongrass to the pot along with the stock, ginger, jalapeños, fish sauce, and brown sugar. Stir until the sugar has dissolved, and then bring the sauce up to a simmer, and simmer for 1 minute. Stir in the coconut milk and simmer until it has reduced by a third and is beginning to thicken, 5 minutes.

4. Add the clams, cover, and cook on low pressure for 1 minute. Release the pressure manually. Discard any clams that didn't open. Taste the sauce, and season it with salt and pepper to taste.

5. Serve the clams in bowls, spooning some broth over them and garnishing with the scallion, cilantro, and a squeeze of lime juice

VIETNAMESE CARAMEL SALMON

TIME: 25 MINUTES

YIELD: 4 SERVINGS

———

1 tablespoon coconut oil, melted, or 1 tablespoon extra-virgin olive oil

⅓ cup packed light brown sugar

3 tablespoons Asian fish sauce

1½ tablespoons soy sauce

1 teaspoon grated peeled fresh ginger

Finely grated zest of 1 lime

Juice of ½ lime

½ teaspoon freshly ground black pepper

4 skinless salmon fillets, preferably center-cut pieces, 6 to 8 ounces each

Sliced scallions (white and green parts), for garnish

Fresh cilantro leaves, for garnish

———

Searing salmon in a tangy lime and ginger caramel that's spiked with Asian fish sauce is one of my favorite ways to cook the fish. Usually I make this in a skillet, starting it on the stovetop and finishing it in the oven. But it cooks beautifully and very quickly in the pressure cooker, turning wonderfully tender. If you like your salmon slightly rare in the center, seek out thick center-cut fillets. They are less likely to overcook than are thinner pieces.

———

1. Using the sauté function, whisk together the oil, brown sugar, fish sauce, soy sauce, ginger, lime zest and juice, and black pepper in the pressure cooker. Bring to a simmer and then turn off the heat.

2. Place the fish in the pressure cooker, skin-side up (if there is skin still attached, that is). Spoon the sauce over the fish, cover, and cook on low pressure for 1 minute. Let the pressure release naturally for 5 minutes; then release the remaining pressure manually. Check the fish for doneness by cutting into one of the fillets. If you prefer your salmon more well-done, cook it for another minute using the sauté function.

3. Carefully lift the salmon fillets onto a serving platter, flipping them over so the browned caramelized side is facing up. Reduce the sauce on the sauté function until it is thick and syrupy, about 3 minutes. Spoon the sauce over the salmon and garnish it with the scallions and cilantro.

TUNA CONFIT
WITH ROSEMARY
+ GARLIC

TIME: 30 MINUTES,
PLUS AT LEAST 1 HOUR MARINATING
YIELD: 4 SERVINGS
GF (WITHOUT THE BREAD) •
P (WITHOUT THE BREAD)

———

2 tablespoons extra-virgin olive oil, plus up to 1 cup more for covering the tuna

2 teaspoons finely chopped fresh rosemary or sage

Finely grated zest of 1 lemon

2 garlic cloves, smashed

½ teaspoon kosher salt

½ teaspoon freshly ground black pepper

½ teaspoon fennel seeds, crushed (optional)

4 6-ounce tuna steaks

Coarse sea salt, for serving

Lemon wedges, for serving

Crusty bread, for serving

———

COOK IT SLOW

———

Cook the tuna on high for 30 minutes
to 1 hour or low for 1 to 2 hours.

Making a confit is my favorite way to cook tuna. When the fish is covered in herbed olive oil and gently poached, it emerges velvety and flavorful. I like to cook this on the rarer side if I'm serving it as an entrée, or a little more done if I plan to use it for tuna salads. Directions for both are below. You can make this well in advance. Covered in the oil used for poaching and stored in the fridge, it will last for at least a week.

———

1. In a medium bowl, combine the oil, rosemary, lemon zest, garlic, salt, pepper, and fennel seeds. Add the tuna and toss to combine; then cover and let marinate in the refrigerator for at least 1 hour and up to 24 hours.

2. Pour 1 cup of water into the pressure cooker and place the steamer rack inside. Transfer the tuna to a 1-quart soufflé dish (do not use a metal dish here), leaving space between the pieces if possible. Pour in enough olive oil to cover the tuna, cover the dish with aluminum foil, and place it on the steamer rack. Cook on low pressure for 5 minutes for a rare center, or 6 to 7 minutes to cook through. Release the pressure manually, remove the lid, and let cool for 20 minutes in the pot.

3. Lift the soufflé dish out of the pressure cooker and place it on a wire rack. Remove the foil and use a slotted spoon to transfer the tuna to a serving platter. Sprinkle the tuna with sea salt and serve it with lemon wedges and crusty bread. (Save the oil and use it to drizzle on bread, pasta, roasted vegetables, or for cooking. Keep it covered and refrigerated for up to 1 week.)

SPANISH GARLICKY
SQUID +
CHORIZO

TIME: 25 MINUTES

YIELD: 3 TO 4 SERVINGS

GF • P

1½ pounds cleaned squid, cut into rings, large tentacles halved

2 tablespoons extra-virgin olive oil

3 ounces cured chorizo, diced (about ⅔ cup)

3 fat garlic cloves, thinly sliced

Kosher salt and freshly ground black pepper, to taste

½ cup fresh parsley, chopped

Finely grated lemon zest (optional)

Flaky sea salt, to taste

Lemon wedges, for serving

Cooking squid in the pressure cooker takes all the anxiety out of its preparation, with the flesh turning out perfectly tender and supple without ever becoming rubbery. Serve this over rice (see page 84) or with some crusty bread to mop up the salty, garlicky, pork-flavored pan juices, which might just be the best part. Be sure to use cured Spanish chorizo here, not the fresh kind found in butcher shops.

---

1. Lay the squid pieces on a dish towel to dry while you prepare the chorizo.

2. Using the sauté function, heat the oil in the pressure cooker. Stir in the chorizo and cook until it starts to crisp, about 5 minutes. Using a slotted spoon, transfer half of the chorizo to a paper-towel-lined plate and set it aside. Stir the garlic into the pressure cooker, and cook until fragrant, about 1 minute. Stir in the squid and a pinch of salt and pepper. Cover and cook on low pressure for 1 minute, and then release the pressure manually.

3. Use a slotted spoon to transfer the squid to a serving platter, and toss it with the parsley and reserved chorizo. For a bright, clean flavor to finish, top with grated lemon zest. For a more intense, smoky flavor, after removing the squid, reduce the sauce in the pressure cooker on the sauté function until thick, 5 to 10 minutes. Strain, and serve the sauce on the side. Top either version with flaky sea salt, and serve lemon wedges on the side.

GRAINS
+
PASTA

GUIDELINES FOR BROWN + WHITE RICE

TIME: 30 TO 35 MINUTES FOR WHITE RICE,
50 TO 60 MINUTES FOR BROWN RICE
YIELD: ABOUT 3 CUPS WHITE RICE
OR 4 CUPS BROWN RICE
ABOUT 6 OR 8 SERVINGS, RESPECTIVELY

The secret to making perfect rice in the electric pressure cooker is to let it steam under a dish towel draped over the top after the lid is removed. The towel absorbs the excess moisture, which helps the grains stay separate instead of clumping together.

You'll notice that I give a range of times for each variety of rice. Deciding whether to cook it more or less depends on many factors, including how soft you like your rice (cook it longer for softer rice), how old your rice is (older, drier rice might need a bit more time), and also your specific brand of pressure cooker. If you're unsure, cook the rice for the shortest time given, and then, if necessary, cook it again for another minute or two.

After you experiment once or twice, you should be able to land on a foolproof method that works for you. My advice is to write it down so you remember what you did for the next time.

White rice, short-grain (such as Arborio, sushi rice, Valencia): Rinse the rice in a fine-mesh sieve until the water runs clear. In the pressure cooker, combine 1 cup rice, 1¼ cups water, and ¼ teaspoon fine sea salt. Cook on high pressure for 3 to 5 minutes; then let the pressure release naturally for 10 minutes. Release the remaining pressure manually. Fluff the rice with a fork, cover the pot with a dish towel, and put the lid back on top of the towel (loosely—don't lock it in) or place a plate on top of the dish towel. Let the rice rest for 10 minutes before serving.

White rice, long-grain (such as basmati or jasmine): Rinse the rice in a fine-mesh sieve until the water runs clear. In the pressure cooker, combine 1 cup rice, 1¼ cups water, and ¼ teaspoon fine sea salt. Cook on high pressure for 8 to 10 minutes; then let the pressure release naturally. Fluff the rice with a fork, cover the pot with a dish towel, and put the lid back on top of the towel (loosely—don't lock it in) or place a plate on top of the dish towel. Let the rice rest for 10 minutes before serving.

GARLIC RICE

TIME: 20 MINUTES
YIELD: 4 SERVINGS
GF • V • VEG

oil

3 to 4 garlic cloves, smashed

1½ cups short-grain white rice, rinsed until the water runs clear

1 teaspoon kosher salt

Brown rice, short-grain: In the pressure cooker, combine 1 cup rice, 1¼ cups water, and ¼ teaspoon fine sea salt. Cook on high pressure for 22 to 24 minutes; then let the pressure release naturally. Fluff the rice with a fork, cover the pot with a dish towel, and put the lid back on top of the towel (loosely—don't lock it in) or place a plate on top of the dish towel. Let the rice rest for 10 minutes before serving.

Brown basmati or other long-grain: In the pressure cooker, combine 1 cup rice, 1¼ cups water, and ¼ teaspoon fine salt. Cook on high pressure for 20 to 22 minutes; then let the pressure release naturally for 10 minutes. Release the remaining pressure manually. Fluff the rice with a fork, cover the pot with a dish towel, and put the lid back on top of the towel (loosely—don't lock it in) or place a plate on top of the dish towel. Let the rice rest for 10 minutes before serving.

You can use any short-grain white rice here—anything from Arborio to sushi rice will work in this quick-cooking, gently garlicky recipe. Because the garlic is smashed but not chopped, it adds a complex, sweet flavor rather than a lot of pungency. For something more intense, feel free to mince some or all of the garlic instead of just smashing it, which will bring out more of its flavor, and leave it in the pot while the rice cooks. For a bit of color, chopped soft herbs—parsley, cilantro, or basil—make a fresh and pretty addition (add them after cooking). Or stir thawed frozen peas or edamame into the hot cooked rice before serving.

1. Using the sauté function, on low if available, let the oil heat up for 30 seconds in the pressure cooker. Then add the garlic and sauté until lightly golden, 2 to 4 minutes.

2. Remove the garlic (reserve it if you want to add it later), and stir in the rice and salt. Add 1½ cups of water. Cover and cook on high pressure for 3 minutes (or use the rice setting).

3. Let the pressure release naturally for 10 minutes, and then release the remaining pressure manually. Fluff the rice as needed. If you like, you can chop up the browned garlic and stir it back into the rice.

CREAMY MACARONI + CHEESE

TIME: 30 MINUTES

YIELD: 4 SERVINGS

VEG

---

2 tablespoons unsalted butter, softened

2 cups whole milk, plus more as needed

¼ cup heavy cream

6 ounces cream cheese, softened

1 garlic clove (optional)

1 teaspoon dry mustard powder

¾ teaspoon kosher salt

¼ teaspoon freshly ground black pepper

⅛ teaspoon cayenne pepper

Pinch of grated nutmeg

8 ounces macaroni pasta

8 ounces grated sharp or extra-sharp cheddar cheese

Why make macaroni and cheese in an electric pressure cooker when it's so easy to do on the stove? You're not necessarily going to save any time with this method, but cooking it all in one pot does make things more convenient. Plus, the cream cheese in the sauce makes this version particularly rich and creamy.

---

1. Brush 1 tablespoon of the butter over the bottom of the pressure cooker.

2. In a blender, blend the milk, cream, cream cheese, remaining 1 tablespoon butter, garlic, dry mustard, salt, pepper, cayenne, and nutmeg.

3. Add the cream cheese mixture and the macaroni to the pressure cooker, and stir to combine. Cover and cook on high pressure for 6 minutes.

4. Release the pressure manually. Stir the noodles, and if they look dry, stir in more milk to taste. If the noodles are too al dente to your liking, stir in the cheddar, then cover and let the pot sit for 5 to 10 minutes; the noodles will cook a little more just sitting in the pot. Otherwise, stir in the cheese and serve immediately.

WILD MUSHROOM, PANCETTA + PEA
RISOTTO

TIME: 45 MINUTES

YIELD: 4 SERVINGS

GF (USING HOMEMADE CHICKEN
STOCK, PAGE 114)

———————

2 tablespoons extra-virgin olive oil

4 ounces pancetta or bacon, diced

8 ounces wild or exotic mushrooms,
such as maitake, chanterelles, oyster
mushrooms, or black trumpets, chopped

2 garlic cloves, thinly sliced

About 3½ to 3¾ cups chicken stock,
preferably homemade (page 114)

1½ cups Arborio rice

1¾ teaspoons kosher salt

¼ cup dry white wine

½ cup fresh or frozen peas,
thawed if frozen

Chopped fresh chives or parsley,
for serving

Freshly grated Parmesan cheese,
for serving (optional)

———————

If you love risotto, that is reason alone to own an electric pressure cooker, because it makes a rather labor-intensive dish extremely fast and simple. Here, the risotto is flavored with browned mushrooms, pancetta, and sweet green peas. If you can't get good wild (also called exotic) mushrooms, use any mushroom that's available to you. The risotto will still be delicious.

———————

1. Using the sauté function, heat 1 tablespoon of the oil in the pressure cooker. Add the pancetta and cook until golden and crisp, 7 to 10 minutes. Using a slotted spoon, transfer the pancetta to a paper-towel-lined plate.

2. Add the mushrooms to the pot and sauté until they've released their liquid and are just browned, about 7 minutes. Stir in the garlic and cook until fragrant, 1 minute. Using a slotted spoon, transfer the mushrooms and garlic to a 4-cup measuring cup, and then add enough stock to make 4 cups.

3. Heat the remaining 1 tablespoon oil in the pressure cooker, stir in the rice and salt, and cook until the rice is lightly toasted, 3 to 5 minutes. Stir in the wine and cook until it has evaporated, about 1 minute. Stir in the mushroom stock mixture and half of the cooked pancetta. Cover and cook on high pressure for 6 minutes.

4. Release the pressure manually. Then stir in the peas and continue stirring until the risotto is creamy and the peas are cooked, about 2 minutes. Taste, adjust the seasonings if necessary, and sprinkle with the reserved crispy pancetta, chives, and Parmesan before serving.

SAFFRON RISOTTO

TIME: 35 MINUTES

YIELD: 4 SERVINGS

GF • VEG (USING HOMEMADE VEGETABLE
BROTH, PAGE 115)

———

2 tablespoons extra-virgin olive oil

2 tablespoons unsalted butter

1 large onion, diced

1 garlic clove, grated on a Microplane
or minced

1½ cups Arborio rice

1½ teaspoons kosher salt

Large pinch of saffron threads

¼ cup dry white wine

4 cups chicken stock or vegetable broth,
preferably homemade (page 114)

¼ cup freshly grated Parmesan cheese

———

This risotto may be the classic accompaniment to Osso Buco (page 48), but don't stop there. Its buttery, earthy flavor and creamy texture make it a special side dish for any braised or roasted meat or fowl. Try it the next time you roast a chicken or grill a steak. It will elevate a simple family meal into a deluxe, company-worthy one. To make this vegetarian, substitute vegetable broth for chicken stock.

———

1. Using the sauté function, heat the oil and 1 tablespoon of the butter in the pressure cooker. Stir in the onion and cook until it is soft, about 5 minutes. Stir in the garlic, cook for 30 seconds, and then stir in the rice and salt. Cook, stirring frequently, until the rice is starting to brown, about 5 minutes.

2. Grind the saffron with a mortar and pestle and add it to the pot. Then pour the wine into the mortar to rinse out any clinging saffron, and pour that into the pot as well. Stir until the wine has been absorbed, about 1 minute.

3. Stir in the stock, cover, and cook on high pressure for 6 minutes; then release the pressure manually. Stir in the Parmesan and continue stirring until the rice has absorbed the rest of the liquid and the risotto is creamy, 1 to 3 minutes. Taste, adjust the seasonings if necessary, and serve.

WILD RICE SALAD WITH CLEMENTINES + PINE NUTS

TIME: 1 HOUR 40 MINUTES

YIELD: 4 TO 6 SERVINGS

GF • P • V • VEG

½ cup pine nuts

1 cup wild rice

2 teaspoons kosher salt, plus more to taste

3 to 4 clementines

½ cup unsweetened dried cherries or unsweetened dried cranberries

2 tablespoons extra-virgin olive oil, plus more for drizzling

2 tablespoons apple cider vinegar

2 scallions (white and green parts), chopped

Freshly ground black pepper, to taste

2 tablespoons chopped fresh cilantro

Flaky sea salt, for garnish (optional)

This is a crunchy, nutty, hearty salad filled with juicy bits of clementine and sweet dried cherries. If you like, you can substitute other nuts for the pine nuts. Chopped pecans or walnuts are especially nice here.

---

1. Using the sauté setting, toast the pine nuts in the dry pressure cooker pot until the nuts release their oil and deepen in color, 2 to 3 minutes, stirring occasionally. Transfer them to a plate to cool.

2. Add the rice, 1¼ cups water, and 1 teaspoon of the salt to the pot, cover it, and cook on high pressure for 30 minutes. (Don't use the rice setting; depending on the machine it may overcook the rice.)

3. Meanwhile, peel 2 of the clementines and separate the sections. Cut each section in half or into thirds and place them in a large bowl. Squeeze the juice from another clementine. You'll need 2 tablespoons; if it's a bit shy, squeeze the fourth clementine as well. Add the 2 tablespoons clementine juice to the bowl containing the clementine sections, and mix in the cherries, olive oil, vinegar, scallions, remaining 1 teaspoon salt, and pepper to taste.

4. When the rice is done, release the pressure manually. Drain the rice in a sieve (there won't be much excess water), and then add it, still warm, to the bowl containing the clementines and toss to combine. It's best if the salad is left for an hour to allow the flavors to meld.

5. Transfer the salad to a serving platter, drizzle it with more olive oil, and garnish with the pine nuts, cilantro, and flaky sea salt.

CLASSIC POLENTA

TIME: 35 MINUTES

YIELD: 4 SERVINGS

GF • VEG (USING WATER OR HOMEMADE
VEGETABLE BROTH, PAGE 115)

———

**5 cups water or chicken stock
(or a combination), plus more as needed**

**1½ cups coarse or medium polenta or
cornmeal, preferably stone-ground**

**¾ teaspoon fine sea salt,
plus more to taste**

1 bay leaf (optional)

**3 tablespoons unsalted butter
or olive oil**

———

COOK IT SLOW

Cook the polenta on high for
2 to 2½ hours or low for 3 to 4 hours,
stirring very occasionally.

All told, the pressure cooker isn't necessarily a faster way to cook polenta, but it is convenient and a lot less work because you don't have to stir the molten mixture as it bubbles, threatening to splatter your forearms. Bear in mind that cooked polenta thickens as it sits, so be prepared to thin it down with a little hot water, stock, or milk depending on the consistency you want for serving.

———

1. Stir all the ingredients together in the pressure cooker and cook on high pressure for 15 minutes.

2. Allow the pressure to release naturally, and then uncover and stir vigorously to break up the clumps. Before serving, let the polenta sit for 5 to 10 minutes to fully absorb the liquid. If it seems too thick, thin it down with a bit more hot water, milk, or stock.

GREEN PERSIAN RICE
WITH TAHDIG

TIME: 1 HOUR

YIELD: 8 SERVINGS

GF · VEG

---

2 cups basmati rice

5 cups packed fresh soft herbs and tender stems (use as many kinds as possible, such as a combination of fresh dill, cilantro, parsley, fennel fronds, tarragon, mint, basil, chervil, and chives)

5 tablespoons unsalted butter: 1 tablespoon softened, 4 tablespoons melted

1 tablespoon dried dill

1½ teaspoons kosher salt, plus more as needed

⅛ teaspoon saffron threads

4 tablespoons extra-virgin olive oil

Filled with herbs and seasoned with aromatic saffron butter, this green and orange–flecked rice dish is magnificent, made even more so by its crunchy, buttery, golden bottom crust called a *tahdig*. Creating the tahdig, which requires a stint on the sauté setting after the rice and herbs are cooked under pressure, takes some practice and finessing, so don't be upset if it doesn't work out perfectly the first time. There's an art to knowing when to take the pot off the heat. If some of the crust sticks to the pot, just scrape it out and lay it on top of the rice for serving. Then make sure everyone gets at least a small piece of it to savor. Those of you with nonstick pots in your pressure cookers will have a much easier time unmolding this. But stainless steel pot owners, fear not; if you're nervous, err on the side of undercooking the tahdig. Better lightly golden than burnt. In any case, with all the saffron and herbs, it will still be delicious. And when you do eventually turn out a perfect version, be prepared for the oohs and aahs. They will be copious. This is a dish worth mastering.

---

1. Rinse the rice in a fine-mesh sieve for several minutes, until the water runs clear; then transfer it to a medium bowl. Cover the rice with warm water and let it sit while you prepare the herbs.

2. Place the herbs, with any tender stems, in a food processor and pulse until finely chopped. (Or you can do this by hand with a knife.) You should have about 2½ cups finely chopped herbs.

3. Brush the bottom of the pressure cooker with the 1 tablespoon softened butter. Drain the rice, and then sprinkle one third of the rice over the bottom of the pot. Top with half of the chopped herbs, ½ tablespoon of the dried dill, and ¼ teaspoon of the salt. Layer another third of the rice on top, and repeat the herb, dill, and salt layers. Top with the remaining rice and then pour in 2 cups of water.

RECIPE CONTINUES

4. Cover and cook on high pressure for 4 minutes. Release the pressure manually, remove the lid, drape a clean kitchen towel on top of the pot, and loosely replace the lid or place a large plate on top. Let the rice sit for 10 minutes.

5. Meanwhile, grind the saffron in a mortar and pestle. Pour 2 tablespoons of the oil into the mortar, swirl it around, and then pour the saffron oil into a measuring cup with a spout. Repeat with the remaining 2 tablespoons oil, scraping the mortar to get every last bit of saffron. Stir the melted butter into the saffron oil.

6. Remove the kitchen towel from the pot. Using the handle of a wooden spoon, poke holes through the rice all the way to the bottom. Pour the butter mixture over the rice, being generous in the center (most pressure cookers tend to have bottoms that slope down from the center, so the butter will slide to the sides). Turn on the sauté function and cook until the rice is browned and crispy on the bottom, 8 to 12 minutes.

7. Turn the pressure cooker off and use a rubber spatula to loosen the rice around the sides and at the bottom of the pot. Remove the pressure cooker pot (using oven mitts or kitchen towels—the pot will be hot). Invert a large platter on top of the pot, and then quickly flip them over together so the rice falls onto the platter, crunchy side up. Or, if you're hesitant to do that, simply scoop the rice onto the platter so that the crunchy side is on top.

FARRO PILAF
WITH SPICED CAULIFLOWER, PINE NUTS + RAISINS

TIME: 1 HOUR

YIELD: 4 TO 6 SERVINGS

VEG

FOR THE FARRO

3 tablespoons extra-virgin olive oil

1 teaspoon garam masala

1¼ teaspoons kosher salt, plus more to taste

½ head cauliflower

⅓ cup white wine vinegar

1 tablespoon honey

⅓ cup golden raisins

1½ cups semi-pearled farro

If made conventionally on the stovetop, this recipe would use three separate pots. But here all the ingredients—the farro, the garam masala–infused cauliflower, and the sweet-and-sour raisins—are all cooked at once, albeit separately, in the pressure cooker. The farro goes in the bottom; the cauliflower sits on top on the steamer rack, and the raisins simmer in a mix of honey and vinegar in a ramekin alongside. When they are all combined with loads of fresh parsley and mint, it's a toothsome, delightfully complex dish that works either as a stunning side dish or as a light meal unto itself.

If you want to cook the farro by itself, pressure-cook it for 9 minutes instead of 8.

---

1. In a medium bowl, combine 2 tablespoons of the oil, the garam masala, and ¼ teaspoon of the salt. Halve the cauliflower from top to bottom, toss with the garam masala mixture until coated, and then wrap the pieces together in one piece of aluminum foil, making sure that you don't put the flat edges of the cauliflower against each other (this would slow down the cooking).

2. In a small ramekin, combine the vinegar, honey, raisins, and a pinch of salt; cover the top with foil.

3. Using the sauté function, heat the remaining 1 tablespoon oil in the pressure cooker. Stir in the farro and remaining 1 teaspoon salt, and cook until the farro smells nutty, about 3 minutes.

4. Stir in 3 cups of water, and then insert the steamer rack on top of the farro. Place the cauliflower and the covered ramekin next to each other on the steamer rack. Cover and cook on high pressure for 8 minutes.

RECIPE CONTINUES

2 teaspoons fresh lime juice

1 small garlic clove, grated on a Microplane or minced

½ teaspoon kosher salt

¼ teaspoon freshly ground black pepper

¼ cup extra-virgin olive oil

TO SERVE

½ cup fresh parsley, chopped

½ cup fresh mint, chopped

¼ cup pine nuts or slivered almonds, toasted

Extra-virgin olive oil to taste

———

5. Meanwhile, make the dressing: In a large bowl, whisk together the lime juice, garlic, salt, and pepper. Whisk in the oil, and set aside.

6. Let the pressure release naturally for 5 minutes, and then release any remaining pressure manually. Transfer the cauliflower to a cutting board and remove the foil. Transfer the ramekin to the counter; remove the foil. Remove the steamer rack, and drain the farro in a strainer over the sink.

7. Measure out 2 teaspoons of the raisin cooking liquid and add that to the bowl containing the dressing. Use a slotted spoon to transfer the raisins to the bowl (save the remaining raisin liquid for drizzling later). Toss the warm farro with the dressing and raisins.

8. Cut the cauliflower into bite-size pieces and add them to the farro. Toss in the parsley, mint, and pine nuts. Taste, and adjust the seasoning if necessary, adding more salt and a drizzle of raisin cooking liquid to taste (the raisin cooking liquid is sweet and sour and wonderful—it really adds zest to the farro). Serve warm or at room temperature, drizzled with olive oil.

BEANS

MOROCCAN CHICKPEAS + KALE

TIME: 2 HOURS

YIELD: 6 TO 8 SERVINGS

V · VEG

———

3 tablespoons olive oil

2 Spanish onions, chopped

1 fennel bulb, diced
(save the fronds for garnish)

1 large jalapeño pepper,
seeded if desired, chopped

4 garlic cloves, minced

1 teaspoon grated peeled fresh ginger

2½ teaspoons kosher salt,
plus more to taste

1 teaspoon ground turmeric

1 teaspoon sweet paprika

¾ teaspoon ground cinnamon

½ teaspoon ground cumin

½ teaspoon freshly ground black pepper

Pinch of cayenne pepper

2 tablespoons tomato paste

1 pound dried chickpeas

1 bunch fresh kale, stems discarded,
leaves torn into bite-size pieces,
about 5 cups

⅔ cup diced dried apricots

2 tablespoons chopped preserved lemon,
or more to taste

½ cup chopped fresh cilantro,
plus more for garnish

———

Full of spices, fresh ginger, and sweet dried apricots, this is a spunky and highly fragrant stew. The kale gives it enough vegetable matter to make it a one-pot meal, and the chickpeas are velvety and satisfying. If you don't have preserved lemons, season this with plenty of fresh lemon juice to balance the sweetness of the cinnamon and apricots.

———

1. Using the sauté function, heat the oil in the pressure cooker. Add the onions, fennel, and jalapeño and sauté until soft, about 10 minutes. Add the garlic, ginger, salt, turmeric, paprika, cinnamon, cumin, black pepper, and cayenne and sauté until they release their fragrance, about 2 minutes. Add the tomato paste and sauté for another minute, until darkened but not burned. (If the tomato paste turns too dark too quickly, turn off the heat.)

2. Add the chickpeas and 5½ cups of water. Cover, and cook on high pressure for 50 minutes; then let the pressure release naturally. If the chickpeas aren't cooked through, cook on high pressure for 5 minutes, then manually release the pressure.

3. Stir in the kale, apricots, and preserved lemon. Using the sauté function, simmer until the kale is wilted, about 5 minutes. Stir in cilantro. Season with more salt if desired, and serve garnished with more cilantro and reserved fennel fronds.

INDIAN CHICKPEAS WITH TOMATOES + ONIONS (CHANA MASALA)

TIME: 1 HOUR 30 MINUTES

YIELD: 6 SERVINGS

V • VEG

———

1 pound dried chickpeas

2½ teaspoons kosher salt

3 onions: 1 halved, 2 thinly sliced

1 bay leaf

3 tablespoons grapeseed, safflower, or peanut oil

4 garlic cloves, grated on a Microplane or minced

1 1½-inch piece fresh ginger, peeled and finely grated

1 jalapeño or other green chile, seeded if desired, minced, plus more for serving

1 tablespoon tomato paste

1 14.5-ounce can diced tomatoes

1 teaspoon garam masala

¾ teaspoon ground cumin

½ teaspoon chili powder

¼ teaspoon ground turmeric

———

This very classic Indian dish features soft chickpeas simmered in a spicy tomato gravy. Here, the dish is made entirely in the pressure cooker, beginning with the dried chickpeas and ending with the bubbling sauce. However, if it's more convenient, you can just cook the chickpeas in the pressure cooker, preparing the sauce and finishing the dish in a skillet. That will leave your pressure cooker free for rice (see page 84), which is just perfect to serve underneath a pile of these fragrant, ruddy chickpeas.

———

1. In the pressure cooker, combine the chickpeas, 7 cups of water, 2 teaspoons of the salt, the onion halves, and the bay leaf. Cover, and cook on high pressure for 40 minutes. Allow the pressure to release naturally. If the chickpeas aren't done, cook at high pressure for another 5 minutes, then manually release the pressure. Drain the chickpeas, reserving the broth, and return the empty pot to the pressure cooker.

2. Using the sauté function (or do this in a skillet over heat), heat the oil in the pressure cooker. Add the sliced onions and cook, stirring frequently, until golden brown, 10 to 15 minutes.

3. Stir in the garlic, ginger, jalapeño, and tomato paste, and cook until fragrant, another minute. Then stir in the tomatoes, scraping any browned bits from the bottom of the pot, and cook until the sauce has thickened, 1 to 3 minutes.

4. Stir in the garam masala, cumin, chili powder, turmeric, and remaining ½ teaspoon salt, and cook until fragrant, 1 minute; then stir in the chickpeas. If the mixture looks too thick, add a few tablespoons of the reserved chickpea cooking broth. Simmer for another 5 minutes to let the flavors meld. Then taste, adjust the seasonings if necessary, and serve with more jalapeño on top if you like. Extra reserved chickpea broth can be frozen for up to 3 months and is an excellent substitute for chicken stock.

SMOKY
LENTILS +
SAUSAGE

TIME: 50 MINUTES

YIELD: 2 TO 4 SERVINGS

———

2 tablespoons extra-virgin olive oil,
plus more as needed

12 ounces of your favorite fresh sausage,
pricked all over with a fork

1 onion, diced

¼ teaspoon fine sea salt,
plus more as needed

3 garlic cloves, thinly sliced

½ teaspoon sweet or hot smoked paprika

¼ teaspoon freshly ground black pepper

¼ cup dry red wine

1 cup dried green lentils

2 sprigs fresh thyme

1 teaspoon apple cider vinegar or white
wine vinegar, or more to taste

Chopped fresh chives or parsley,
for serving

Dijon mustard, for serving

———

You can use any type of sausage to top these rich, earthy lentils, which take on a rustic flavor from the smoked paprika in which they're simmered. Pork is the obvious sausage choice here, but turkey or lamb sausages would also work well. Don't overlook the mustard for serving. It gives a nice pop of flavor right at the end.

———

1. Using the sauté function, heat the oil in the pressure cooker until hot. Add the sausage and cook until well browned on all sides, 10 to 15 minutes. Transfer the sausage to a plate.

2. If the pot looks dry, add a drizzle of oil. Add the onion and salt, and cook until the onion has softened, about 5 minutes. Stir in the garlic, paprika, and pepper, and cook for another minute.

3. Stir in the wine, scraping up any browned bits from the bottom of the pot, and then add the lentils, thyme, and 1¾ cups of water. Insert the steamer rack on top of the lentils, and arrange the sausages on the rack.

4. Cover and cook on high pressure for 11 minutes. Allow the pressure to release naturally. Transfer the sausages to a plate and remove the steamer rack. Discard thyme sprigs. Stir the vinegar into the lentils; taste and add more vinegar and/or salt, if needed. Scoop the lentils onto a serving platter and drizzle with olive oil. Slice the sausages and arrange them on top. Garnish with the chives, and serve with the mustard on the side.

HUMMUS

TIME: 1 HOUR 30 MINUTES

YIELD: 3 CUPS

V · VEG

———

8 ounces (1⅓ cups) dried chickpeas

**1½ teaspoons kosher salt,
plus more as needed**

Juice of 1 lemon, plus more as needed

**2 garlic cloves, grated on a Microplane
or chopped**

¼ teaspoon ground cumin

⅓ cup tahini

Ice water, as needed

**2 tablespoons extra-virgin olive oil,
plus more for serving**

Sweet or hot paprika, for serving

———

The pressure cooker is ideal for making hummus because it can cook the chickpeas until they are extremely tender, easy to puree into the silkiest, smoothest of dips. This is a very traditional recipe, seasoned with garlic, lemon, tahini, and just a touch of cumin. Leftovers will last for up to a week in the fridge.

———

1. Pour the chickpeas and 1 teaspoon of the salt into the pressure cooker and add water to cover by 1 inch. Cook on high pressure for 50 minutes. Allow the pressure to release naturally. The chickpeas should be very soft. If not, cook at high pressure for another 5 minutes, then manually release the pressure. Drain the chickpeas.

2. Meanwhile, place the lemon, garlic, cumin, and remaining ½ teaspoon salt in a blender or food processor and let the mixture sit for 5 minutes without processing. Then add the tahini and process to combine; you'll end up with a thick paste. Add 2 tablespoons ice water and blend it in, and then continue adding ice water, 1 tablespoon at a time, blending until the tahini has thinned down to a sauce consistency.

3. Add the drained chickpeas and the olive oil to the tahini and blend to combine, stopping to scrape down the sides of the blender jar as necessary. If the hummus looks too thick, add more ice water, 1 tablespoon at a time. Taste, and adjust the seasoning if necessary. Then scrape the hummus into a serving dish and top it with a generous drizzle of olive oil and a liberal sprinkling of paprika.

YELLOW SPLIT PEA
DHAL WITH CUMIN + GINGER

TIME: 45 MINUTES
YIELD: 8 SERVINGS
GF · V · VEG

---

1 pound dried yellow split peas,
picked over and rinsed

1½ teaspoons fine sea salt,
plus more to taste

1 bay leaf

¼ cup coconut oil, grapeseed oil,
or peanut oil

4 scallions, white and green parts
separated and thinly sliced

1 jalapeño pepper, seeded if desired,
thinly sliced

1 teaspoon finely grated peeled
fresh ginger

1 teaspoon cumin seeds

½ teaspoon garam masala

½ teaspoon freshly cracked black pepper

COOK IT SLOW

Cook on high for 6 to 7 hours or
low for 8 to 10 hours.

In many dhal recipes, the beans or legumes are cooked with very little seasoning, then drizzled with a piquant homemade spice oil just before serving. You can vary the spice oil, called a *tarka*, to taste, adding any combination of chiles, spices, and allium that you like. Thinly sliced garlic and/or shallots or onions can replace the scallions here, and dried red chiles or a pinch of chile flakes can stand in for the fresh green chile. As for the spices, the options are as varied as your spice cabinet. Have fun changing the flavors to suit your taste and mood.

You'll notice that I give a range for the amount of water; it depends upon how thick or thin you prefer your dhal. Five cups gives you a medium-thick, porridge-like dhal, while six cups will give you something soupier. Note that the dhal will continue to thicken up quite a lot as it sits. If it gets too thick, you can always add a little more hot water to thin it out. Dhal is forgiving that way.

---

1. Put the split peas into the pressure cooker along with the salt, bay leaf, and 5 to 6 cups of water, depending on how soupy you like your dhal (see headnote). Cover, and cook on high pressure for 20 minutes. Let the pressure release naturally. If the peas aren't cooked through, cook on high pressure for 5 minutes, then release pressure manually.

2. Meanwhile, in a skillet, heat the oil until hot, and then add the scallion whites (save the greens for garnish), jalapeño, and ginger. Cook until everything turns golden, 3 to 5 minutes. Then add the cumin seeds, garam masala, and pepper and cook for 1 to 2 minutes longer, until fragrant.

3. To serve, spoon the split peas into bowls and top with some of the spice oil, the scallion greens, and a sprinkling of salt to taste.

BLACK BEANS
WITH GREEN CHILES + CUMIN

TIME: 2 HOURS

YIELD: 6 TO 8 SERVINGS

GF • V (WITHOUT THE CHEESE) • VEG

---

3 poblano chiles

2 jalapeño or serrano chiles

5 tablespoons extra-virgin olive oil

1 large onion, diced

2 tablespoons finely chopped fresh sage
(or use marjoram or oregano)

3 garlic cloves, minced

1 teaspoon chili powder

1 teaspoon ground cumin

1 pound dried black beans

1 tablespoon kosher salt,
plus more as needed

1 medium-size ripe tomato, quartered

1 bunch fresh cilantro, stems and
leaves separated

1 small bunch scallions, white and green
parts separated, thinly sliced

Freshly ground black pepper, to taste

Grated Monterey Jack cheese, for serving
(optional)

Lime wedges, for serving

COOK IT SLOW

Cook on high for 6 to 7 hours or on low for
8 to 10 hours. Add the tomato puree
during the last 20 minutes.

These soft and spicy beans are a lot like the best possible version of a vegetarian chili, with earthy black beans standing in for the usual pinto or kidney beans. The roasted green chiles add both smokiness and heat, and are worth the extra steps of charring and peeling. Serve this over rice (page 84) or Garlic Rice (page 85), or with warm tortillas.

---

1. Roast the poblano and jalapeño chiles over an open flame on your stove, or under your broiler, until their skins are blistered and charred all over, about 10 minutes. Transfer them to a bowl, cover with a plate, and let them sit until they are cool enough to handle. Then rub the skins off with a paper towel, and seed and dice the chiles.

2. Using the sauté function, heat 2 tablespoons of the oil in the pressure cooker. Stir in the onion and cook until golden, about 15 minutes. Stir in the sage, two-thirds of the minced garlic, and the chili powder and cumin; cook for 1 minute. Stir in the chopped poblanos, half the jalapeños, and the beans, salt, and 5 cups of water. Cover, and cook on high pressure for 40 minutes. Allow the pressure to release naturally. If the beans aren't cooked through, cook on high pressure for 5 minutes, then manually release pressure.

3. While the beans are cooking, in a blender combine the tomato, cilantro stems, half the cilantro leaves, the scallion whites, the remaining garlic, the remaining 3 tablespoons oil, the remaining jalapeños, and a large pinch of salt. Blend to puree; then taste and add more salt and pepper if necessary.

4. When the beans finish cooking, stir in the tomato puree; let sit for 5 minutes. Then, if the mix seems thin, simmer it on the sauté setting for a few minutes to thicken it up.

5. Transfer the beans to individual serving bowls, and top with the cheese if using, the remaining cilantro leaves, and thinly sliced scallion greens. Serve with lime wedges on the side.

GARLICKY BEANS
WITH BROCCOLI RABE

TIME: 45 MINUTES

YIELD: 8 SERVINGS

GF • V • VEG

**1 pound dried cannellini
or other white beans**

**7 garlic cloves: 4 smashed,
3 thinly sliced**

**4 tablespoons plus ½ cup extra-virgin
olive oil, plus more as needed**

**2½ teaspoons kosher salt,
plus more as needed**

1 large sprig fresh rosemary

1 bay leaf

1 carrot, trimmed

**1 large or 2 small red onions,
halved and thinly sliced**

**1 pound fresh broccoli rabe,
woody ends trimmed**

⅛ teaspoon crushed red pepper flakes

This white bean dish isn't shy when it comes to garlic. It's used in the pot along with the simmering beans, and also fried in olive oil as a crunchy, pungent garnish. As a contrast, the broccoli rabe and red onion get very sweet when you sauté them slowly until they are browned and caramelized. Alongside the soft, mild white beans, it's a satisfying and comforting dish with a garlicky kick.

---

1. In the pressure cooker, combine the beans, 7 cups of water, the 4 smashed garlic cloves, 2 tablespoons of the oil, and 2 teaspoons of the salt. Tie the rosemary, bay leaf, and carrot together with kitchen twine, and then drop the bundle into the pressure cooker. Cover, and cook on high pressure for 25 minutes. Allow the pressure to release naturally. If the beans aren't done, cook on high pressure for another 5 minutes, then manually release the pressure.

2. While the beans are cooking, heat ½ cup oil in a large skillet over medium-low heat. Stir in the sliced garlic and a pinch of salt, and sauté until the garlic is just starting to turn golden, 2 to 3 minutes. Transfer the garlic oil to a small bowl and reserve for the garnish.

3. Return the skillet to the stove, raise the heat to medium-high, and add the remaining 2 tablespoons oil. Stir in the onion and cook until golden, about 5 minutes. Raise the heat to high and stir in the broccoli rabe, remaining ½ teaspoon salt, and the red pepper flakes, tossing to coat with the oil. Add ½ cup of water to the skillet, and cook until the water has been absorbed and the broccoli rabe is softened and browned, about 10 minutes (drizzle in more oil as necessary to prevent sticking).

4. To serve, remove the herb bundle from the bean pot and then drain the beans, reserving the liquid if you like (use it like stock). Place the beans in a shallow bowl or on a platter. Drizzle the beans with the garlic oil, and top with the broccoli rabe.

SOUPS

BONE BROTH
OR
CHICKEN STOCK

TIME: BETWEEN 1 AND 5 HOURS,
DEPENDING ON BONES USED
AND DESIRED RESULT
YIELD: 3 QUARTS
GF • P

---

3 pounds bones, preferably a mix of meaty bones and marrow-filled bones

3 tablespoons apple cider vinegar

1½ tablespoons coarse sea salt, or to taste

1 to 2 celery stalks

1 large carrot

1 large onion, 2 leeks, or a bunch of leek greens

1 whole clove or star anise pod

2 to 6 garlic cloves

5 to 7 sprigs fresh thyme or dill

5 to 7 sprigs fresh parsley

1 bay leaf

1 teaspoon black peppercorns

2 to 4 1-inch-thick coins peeled fresh ginger (optional)

The difference between bone broth and regular broth, or stock, comes down to the length of the cooking time and the addition of acid to the cooking liquid. They taste very similar, though the bone broth has a slightly more intense flavor and a thicker, silkier texture than stock. They can be used interchangeably in recipes.

Really, the main difference is that many people consider bone broth to be therapeutic. The longer cooking time of a bone broth allows the collagen and minerals from the bones and connective tissue to dissolve into the liquid. This process is aided by adding a bit of acid to the pot, which also helps the bones break down (at the end of cooking, the bones should crumble if you press on them).

Bone broths need ample cooking time for all this to occur, at least 24 to 48 hours when simmered conventionally on the stove or in a slow-cooker. Regular stocks cook much more quickly; 2 to 4 hours is all you need on the stove.

But whether you are making bone broth or regular stock, the pressure cooker does the job much faster. Regular stocks will be ready in only an hour or two, while bone broths will be ready in an afternoon.

You can use any bones to make bone broth or stock. I usually use a combination of chicken bones left over from roasted birds (I keep them stored in the freezer) and fresh, meaty pork and beef soup bones that I get from the farmer's market (you can also find them in the supermarket or at a butcher shop). But after the holidays one year, I used a goose carcass, and around Thanksgiving, turkey will likely be the bones of choice. Feel free to mix and match all manner of meat and fowl. Or if you want to make a particular kind of stock—say, chicken or beef—use bones only from that animal.

Roasting the bones before adding them to the pot caramelizes them and makes for a much richer and better-tasting broth. But for a light chicken stock you could skip that step.

---

1. If you want to roast the bones first, heat the oven to 450°F. Lay the bones out on a rimmed baking sheet and roast until well browned, 25 to 35 minutes.

2. Put the bones (roasted or not) in the pressure cooker pot and add all the remaining ingredients. Cover with 3 to 3½ quarts of water (the water shouldn't come more than two-thirds of the way up the side of the pot). To make regular stock, cook on high pressure for 1 hour if using all chicken or poultry bones, or 2 hours for beef or pork bones or a combination of poultry and meat. For bone broth, cook on high pressure for 3 hours for poultry bones, and 4½ hours for beef, pork, or mixed bones. When making bone broth, you'll know you've cooked it long enough if all the connective tissue, tendons, and cartilage have dissolved and the bones crumble a bit when you poke at them. If this hasn't happened, cook it on high pressure for another 30 minutes and check it again.

3. Allow the pressure to release naturally. Strain the broth, discarding the solids. Use the broth or stock right away, or store it in the refrigerator or freezer. Bone broth and regular stock will keep for 5 days refrigerated or up to 6 months frozen.

COOK IT SLOW

Cook on low for 10 to 12 hours for regular stock, and 24 to 48 hours for bone broth.

To make **VEGETABLE BROTH** in the electric pressure cooker, combine 3 sliced onions and/or leeks, 3 sliced carrots, 3 sliced celery stalks with leaves, 2 garlic cloves, 1 halved plum tomato, 1 bay leaf, 1 teaspoon peppercorns, a large pinch of sea salt, 4 parsley sprigs, and a cup or so of mushrooms if you have them. Cover with water by 2 inches, cover, and cook on high pressure for 20 minutes. Allow the pressure to naturally release.

VIETNAMESE CHICKEN + RICE SOUP

TIME: 1 HOUR

YIELD: 4 TO 6 SERVINGS

GF (USING HOMEMADE CHICKEN STOCK, PAGE 114)

---

8 cups chicken stock, preferably homemade (see page 114)

4 skinless, boneless chicken thighs

2 4 x 4-inch pieces dried kombu (see headnote)

1 4-inch-long piece fresh ginger, peeled, sliced into 4 coins, and smashed with the side of a knife

6 star anise pods

1 4-inch cinnamon stick

4 whole cloves

¾ cup sushi or glutinous (sticky) rice

2 tablespoons Asian fish sauce, plus more to taste

2 teaspoons palm sugar or light brown sugar

2 scallions (white and green parts), thinly sliced

2 jalapeño peppers, seeded if desired and thinly sliced

1 cup fresh cilantro leaves with tender stems, coarsely chopped

½ cup thinly sliced white onion

In this pho-like soup, chicken stock is heavily seasoned with ginger, star anise, and cinnamon, and loaded with shredded chicken, soft rice, and plenty of herbs, chiles, and onions for garnish. The combination of flavors is pungent, fresh, and robust, and it has become one of my all-time-favorite chicken soups. The recipe comes from Elizabeth Street Café in Austin, Texas, adapted here to work in the pressure cooker.

Note that the recipe calls for kombu, a type of dried seaweed that's available at Asian markets and health food stores, which adds an umami richness to the stock. But if you can't find it, you can leave it out.

---

1. In the pressure cooker, combine the stock, chicken, kombu, ginger, star anise, cinnamon stick, cloves, and 2 cups of water. Cover, and cook on high pressure for 8 minutes.

2. Meanwhile, rinse the rice in a sieve under cold running water until the water runs clear.

3. Allow the pressure to release naturally for 10 minutes; then release the remaining pressure manually. Using tongs, transfer the chicken to a plate. Remove the solids from the stock with a slotted spoon or a small sieve.

4. Stir the rice, fish sauce, and palm sugar into the stock. Cook on high pressure for 1 minute.

5. Meanwhile, shred the chicken.

6. Allow the pressure to release naturally for 10 minutes; then release the remaining pressure manually. Return the shredded chicken to the pot.

7. Taste, and season the soup with more fish sauce if necessary. Divide the soup among individual bowls. Top with the scallions, jalapeños, cilantro, and onion, and serve.

CHICKEN SOUP
WITH DILL

TIME: 1 HOUR

YIELD: 6 SERVINGS

GF (WITHOUT THE NOODLES; USING HOME-
MADE CHICKEN STOCK, PAGE 114) •
P (WITHOUT THE NOODLES)

---

1 4- to 4½-pound chicken or 4 pounds
bone-in chicken parts

1 quart chicken stock, preferably
homemade (see page 114)

1 to 4 garlic cloves, smashed

1 teaspoon black peppercorns

1 bay leaf

5 large sprigs fresh dill, plus chopped
dill for garnish

3 large sprigs fresh parsley

3 large sprigs fresh thyme

Fine sea salt, as needed

1 to 2 tablespoons unsalted butter,
schmaltz, or olive oil

2 leeks (white and light green parts only),
thinly sliced

2 carrots, thinly sliced

2 celery stalks, sliced

Cooked egg noodles or rice, for serving
(optional)

COOK IT SLOW

Cook on high for 4 to 6 hours or
low for 7 to 9 hours.

With its large chunks of chicken, carrots, and celery and flecks of green dill, this supremely comforting soup will soothe just about any discomfort, physical or otherwise, that ails you. Then, after simmering up a potful, save the leftover chicken bones to make chicken stock so you'll have it on hand for the next batch.

Whenever I make chicken soup, I cook the noodles or rice separately, then add them to the pot just before serving for the clearest broth. However, if you'd rather cook them directly in the soup broth, go ahead and do so on the sauté function after you've removed the chicken (follow package directions to get the noodle timing right; rice will take 12 to 15 minutes).

You'll probably end up with more cooked chicken here than you'll need for the soup. Save it for another meal. I especially love it tossed with garlicky mayonnaise (see page 134) for chicken salad sandwiches.

---

1. Put the chicken in the pressure cooker and cover it with the stock and 1 cup of water. Add the garlic, peppercorns, bay leaf, and the dill, parsley, and thyme sprigs. Cover, and cook on high pressure for 20 minutes. Allow the pressure to release naturally for 15 minutes; then release the remaining pressure manually.

2. Use tongs to remove the chicken from the pot and place it in a large bowl. Strain the broth, discarding the solids. Add salt to taste and set the broth aside.

3. Return the empty pot to the pressure cooker. Using the sauté function, melt the butter; then stir in the leeks and a pinch of salt. Sauté until the leeks are limp and golden at the edges, 3 to 4 minutes.

4. Add the carrots, celery, and reserved broth to the pot. Cook on high pressure for 3 minutes, and then release the pressure manually.

5. While the vegetables are cooking, shred chicken into bite-size pieces (save the bones and skin for stock).

6. To serve, return as much of the shredded chicken to the soup as you like, and add the noodles or rice if using. Top with fresh dill and serve hot.

SPLIT PEA SOUP
WITH HAM HOCKS

TIME: 1 HOUR 15 MINUTES

YIELD: 4 TO 6 SERVINGS

GF (USING HOMEMADE STOCK, PAGE 114)

———

1 tablespoon extra-virgin olive oil

1 pound ham hocks
(2 or 3 1¼-inch-thick hocks),
fresh or smoked

3 celery stalks, finely diced

1 medium onion, diced

3 sprigs fresh thyme

½ teaspoon fine sea salt,
plus more to taste

½ teaspoon freshly ground black pepper

1 pound dried green split peas

1 quart pork, chicken, or vegetable stock,
preferably homemade (see page 114)

⅛ teaspoon grated nutmeg

Fresh lemon juice, for serving

———

COOK IT SLOW

———

Cook on high for 6 to 7 hours or
low for 8 to 10 hours.

You can make this soup either mildly porky or more assertively smoky depending upon what kind of ham hocks you buy. Fresh hocks will give the soup a brawny, meaty flavor, but without the deep, smoky saltiness of the smoked hocks. Both work here, so choose the one that suits your mood.

———

1. Using the sauté function, heat the oil in the pressure cooker. If you are using fresh hocks, sprinkle them all over with salt and sear them until some of the fat is rendered and the meat is browned, about 10 minutes; then transfer them to a plate. Smoked hocks don't need to be salted or seared; do not add them yet.

2. Add the celery, onion, thyme sprigs, salt, and pepper to the pressure cooker and sauté until the vegetables have softened, about 5 minutes.

3. Stir in the split peas, stock, ham hocks, and nutmeg. Cover, and cook on high pressure for 25 minutes.

4. Allow the pressure to release naturally for 20 minutes; then release the remaining pressure manually. If the peas aren't done, cook for another 5 minutes on high pressure, then manually release the pressure. Transfer the ham hocks to a plate and discard the thyme sprigs. Remove the bones, dice or shred the ham into bite-size pieces, and return the meat to the soup.

5. Give the soup a good stir and season it well with salt and pepper to taste. If the soup is too thick, mix in a little water until it has reached the desired consistency. Stir in a little lemon juice to taste before serving.

BUTTERNUT SQUASH SOUP
WITH CORIANDER + LEMON

TIME: 1 HOUR 10 MINUTES
YIELD: 4 TO 6 SERVINGS
GF • V • VEG (USING HOMEMADE
VEGETABLE BROTH, PAGE 115)

---

1 tablespoon extra-virgin olive oil, plus more for serving

2 cups thinly sliced fennel (reserve the fronds for garnish)

1 medium onion, diced

½ teaspoon kosher salt, plus more to taste

1 butternut squash (about 2 pounds), peeled, seeded, and cut into 1-inch cubes

2 teaspoons ground coriander

1 quart vegetable or chicken stock, preferably homemade (see page 114)

Finely grated zest and juice of 1 lemon

Freshly ground black pepper, to taste

1 cup chopped fresh cilantro

COOK IT SLOW

Cook on high for 2 to 3 hours or low for 4 to 5 hours.

If you have an immersion blender, you can blend this creamy, gently sweet soup directly in your pressure cooker, which makes it extremely convenient. I like to finish it with lemon juice and zest, which echoes the lemony-earthy flavor of the coriander. But lime is a bit sharper and a little more floral, and you can easily substitute one citrus for the other. And if you're a rutabaga or parsnip fan, you can swap out those peeled and diced roots, either alone or in combination, for the squash.

---

1. Using the sauté function, heat the oil in the pressure cooker. Add the fennel, onion, and salt, and cook until the vegetables have just softened, 5 minutes. Add the squash and coriander and cook, stirring occasionally, until the vegetables are starting to turn golden at the edges, 7 to 10 minutes.

2. Add the stock, cover, and cook on high pressure for 20 minutes. Let the pressure release naturally.

3. Using an immersion blender directly in the pot or transferring the soup to a blender, puree the soup with the lemon zest until smooth. Season with salt, pepper, and lemon juice to taste. Serve garnished with the fennel fronds, cilantro, and a drizzle of olive oil.

RED LENTIL SOUP
WITH MINT OIL

TIME: 30 MINUTES

YIELD: 2 TO 4 SERVINGS

GF • V • VEG (USING HOMEMADE
VEGETABLE BROTH, PAGE 115)

**4 tablespoons plus ¼ cup
extra-virgin olive oil**

1 onion, chopped

2 garlic cloves, minced

1 tablespoon tomato paste

1 teaspoon ground cumin

**¾ teaspoon kosher salt,
plus more to taste**

½ teaspoon ground turmeric

¼ teaspoon freshly ground black pepper

**Pinch of ancho or New Mexico chile
powder or cayenne pepper,
plus more to taste**

**1 quart chicken or vegetable stock,
preferably homemade (see page 114)**

**½ cup diced tomatoes and their juices
(either canned or fresh)**

1 cup dried red lentils

**½ tablespoon dried mint,
preferably Turkish mint**

Juice of ½ lemon, more to taste

3 tablespoons chopped fresh mint

Flaky sea salt, for serving

A lemony, cumin-scented red lentil soup is one of my go-to recipes, something that I make on chilly days on a regular basis. This version has the addition of homemade mint oil, which adds a delicate herbal flavor. However, I often make the soup without the oil and it's nearly as good, so feel free to leave it out.

---

1. Using the sauté function, heat 3 tablespoons of the oil in the pressure cooker. When it is hot, stir in the onion and sauté until golden, about 5 minutes. Stir in the garlic, tomato paste, cumin, salt, turmeric, black pepper, and chili powder, and cook until fragrant, another 2 minutes.

2. Add the stock, tomatoes, lentils, and 1 tablespoon of the oil to the pot. Cover, and cook on high pressure for 6 minutes. Allow the pressure to release naturally for 10 minutes; then release the remaining pressure manually.

3. Meanwhile, heat the remaining ¼ cup oil in a small saucepan over medium-low heat. Stir in the dried mint, and cook until the mint starts to dance in the pan, about 15 minutes. Remove from the heat and let cool. Reserve the mint oil for garnish.

4. Stir in the lemon juice, adding more to taste, along with more salt and pepper if needed. To serve, ladle the soup into bowls and drizzle with the mint oil, fresh mint, and flaky sea salt to taste.

COOK IT SLOW

Cook for 2 to 3 hours on high
or 4 to 6 on low.

RED CURRY VEGETABLE NOODLE SOUP

TIME: 35 MINUTES

YIELD: 4 TO 6 SERVINGS

GF • V • VEG (USING HOMEMADE
VEGETABLE BROTH, PAGE 115)

---

1 bunch baby bok choy, white stems
separated from green leaves

2 tablespoons safflower or olive oil

1 small onion, diced

2 garlic cloves, minced

1 tablespoon grated peeled fresh ginger

2 tablespoons red curry paste

1 small sweet potato, peeled and
cut into 1-inch pieces

1 quart chicken or vegetable stock,
preferably homemade (see page 114)

2 teaspoons Asian fish sauce

2 teaspoons dark brown sugar

1 13-ounce can full-fat coconut milk
(not refrigerated nondairy beverage)

½ teaspoon kosher salt,
plus more to taste

8 ounces vermicelli rice noodles

2 limes: 1 juiced, 1 cut into wedges

¼ cup coarsely chopped fresh cilantro,
for garnish

A little jar or can of red curry paste is a staple in my kitchen, where I add it to all types of soups, stews, and sautés. Here I use the paste as the base for a gently sweet and mildly spicy Thai-style vegetable soup. For a lighter meal, leave out the noodles.

---

1. Slice the bok choy stems into ½-inch pieces. Slice the leaves into 1-inch pieces. Set aside.

2. Using the sauté function, heat the oil in the pressure cooker. Add the onion, garlic, ginger, and curry paste and cook until fragrant, 1 to 2 minutes. Add the sweet potato and the white stems of the bok choy, along with the stock. Bring to a simmer and add the fish sauce and brown sugar, stirring until the sugar dissolves, about 1 minute.

3. Stir in the coconut milk and salt, cover, and cook on high pressure for 15 minutes.

4. Meanwhile, cook the vermicelli noodles according to the package instructions.

5. Release the pressure manually. Remove the lid and stir in the bok choy greens until wilted. Add the lime juice and more salt to taste.

6. Divide the noodles among individual bowls and ladle the soup on top, garnishing with the cilantro and lime wedges.

FRENCH ONION SOUP

TIME: 30 MINUTES

YIELD: 4 TO 6 SERVINGS

VEG (USING HOMEMADE VEGETABLE
BROTH, PAGE 115)

———

1 tablespoon unsalted butter

1 teaspoon olive oil,
plus more for the croutons

2 large or 3 medium onions, halved and
cut into ¼-inch-thick slices

1 teaspoon kosher salt

1 teaspoon sugar

1 teaspoon all-purpose flour

2 tablespoons dry sherry or white wine

1 quart beef or chicken stock,
preferably homemade (see page 114)

1 sprig fresh thyme

Freshly ground black pepper to taste

French bread, cut into 1-inch-thick slices
(1 slice per serving)

1 garlic clove, halved

1 cup grated Gruyère cheese

———

Full of sweet caramelized onions, heady stock, and gar-licky croutons covered with melted Gruyère, a classic French onion soup is celebration in a bowl, something a lot more fun and festive than your average soup. Use your best homemade stock here if you can—it has so much more flavor and richness than anything store-bought, and in this recipe it will make a difference. Vegetarians can substitute vegetable stock, preferably one made with lots of mushrooms for depth of flavor.

———

1. Using the sauté function, heat the butter and oil in the pressure cooker. Add the onions and season with ½ teaspoon of the salt and the sugar. Cook, stirring often, until the onions are caramelized and a deep golden color, 15 to 20 minutes.

2. Sprinkle in the flour and stir well. Add the sherry and a cup of the stock, scraping up the bits stuck to the bottom of the pot. Add the thyme sprig, the rest of the stock, and the remaining ½ teaspoon salt. Cover, and cook on high pressure for 5 minutes.

3. Meanwhile, turn on the broiler.

4. Place the bread slices on a baking sheet. Toast the bread under the broiler until it is just beginning to take on color, 1 to 2 minutes per side. Remove the baking sheet from the broiler, leaving the broiler on, and rub both sides of each slice with the garlic. Brush the tops of the slices with olive oil, top with the cheese, slide the sheet back under the broiler, and cook until the cheese has melted and is starting to turn golden, 1 to 2 minutes.

5. Release the pressure manually. Remove the thyme sprig, and season the soup with salt and pepper to taste. To serve, place a crouton in each bowl and ladle the soup over it, allowing the bread to soak up the stock.

BEEF BARLEY
VEGETABLE
SOUP

TIME: 1 HOUR 30 MINUTES
YIELD: 4 TO 6 SERVINGS

———————

1½ pounds beef stew meat,
cut into ¾-inch cubes

1½ teaspoons kosher salt,
plus more to taste

1 teaspoon freshly ground black pepper,
plus more to taste

1 tablespoon extra-virgin olive oil

¼ cup dry red wine

2 cups (about 6 ounces) quartered
cremini mushrooms

4 shallots, thinly sliced

3 carrots, sliced into ¼-inch-thick rounds

3 celery stalks, diced into ¼-inch pieces

¾ cup pearl barley

2 sprigs fresh thyme

2 bay leaves

1 quart beef or chicken stock, preferably
homemade (see page 114)

2 tablespoons chopped fresh parsley

Sherry vinegar, to taste

———————

A classic, hearty soup, this is a little more interesting than most versions thanks to a touch of red wine in the stock and sherry vinegar drizzled on top. I also like to make this soup with lamb instead of beef. If you're a lamb lover, give it a try.

———————

1. Season the beef with 1 teaspoon of the salt and ½ teaspoon of the pepper. Using the sauté function, on high if available, heat the oil in the pressure cooker (or use a skillet). Working in batches to avoid overcrowding, brown the meat well on all sides, about 2 to 3 minutes per side. With a slotted spoon, transfer the beef to a bowl.

2. Pour the wine into the pot (or skillet) to deglaze it, using a wooden spoon to scrape up the browned bits stuck to the bottom and sides. Allow the liquid to reduce by half, 2 to 3 minutes.

3. Add the mushrooms, shallots, carrots, and celery and mix well with the reduced wine. Season with the remaining ½ teaspoon salt and ½ teaspoon pepper. Cook until the vegetables release moisture and start to soften, 8 to 10 minutes. Return the beef and any juices to the pot. (If using a skillet, transfer the vegetables from the pan to the pot and add the beef.)

4. Add the barley, thyme sprigs, bay leaves, and stock to the pot. Cover, and cook on high pressure for 30 minutes. Let the pressure release naturally for 15 minutes; then release the remaining pressure manually. Discard the bay leaf and thyme sprigs. Taste, and season with more salt and pepper if needed.

5. Ladle the soup into individual bowls, and garnish with the parsley and a sprinkle of sherry vinegar.

COOK IT SLOW

Cook on high for 5 to 6 hours or low for
7 to 8 hours. Check the soup as it cooks;
it might need up to a cup more liquid
than in the pressure cooker. Add water
or stock as needed.

VEGETABLES

BEETS
WITH DILL, LIME + YOGURT

TIME: 1 HOUR

YIELD: 4 SERVINGS

GF · VEG

———————

6 medium beets (about 1½ pounds)

1 lime

Extra-virgin olive oil, for drizzling

1 cup plain whole-milk yogurt

1 garlic clove, grated on a Microplane or minced

Pinch of fine sea salt

2 tablespoons chopped fresh dill

Flaky sea salt, for garnish

Freshly ground black pepper, for garnish

———————

In this colorful dish, sweet beets are zipped up with lime, yogurt, and garlic. If you only have Greek yogurt on hand, thin it down with a little water or milk; you're looking for a sauce that's thin enough to drizzle. You can use any kind of beets here. Red and candy cane beets are sweeter than yellow beets, but all work wonderfully well. Or use a combination for the most stunning presentation imaginable.

———————

1. Remove any greens and scrub the beets under warm water.

2. Pour 1½ cups of water into the pressure cooker pot. Insert the steamer basket and put the 6 beets in the basket. Cook on high pressure for 30 minutes. Release the pressure manually. Test the beets by piercing them with a fork; they should be tender. If not, cook on high pressure again for another 5 to 10 minutes.

3. Meanwhile, grate the zest off the lime and reserve it; then cut the lime into wedges.

4. When the beets are tender, transfer them to a large bowl and let them cool until you're comfortable handling them. Working quickly, skin the beets while they are still warm (they are harder to peel after they've entirely cooled down). You can use a paring knife to skin them, or rub the skins off with a paper towel.

5. Cut the peeled beets into slices or wedges, and arrange them on a platter. Drizzle with olive oil, and then squeeze some of the fresh lime juice over them.

6. In a small bowl, whisk together the yogurt, garlic, and reserved lime zest. Drizzle the dressing over the beets and top with the dill, flaky sea salt, and lots of black pepper.

TANGERINE CARROTS
WITH RICOTTA, CHIVES + WALNUTS

TIME: 30 MINUTES

YIELD: 4 SERVINGS

GF • VEG

**½ cup walnuts
(or use another type of nut if you prefer)**

**1 pound carrots, halved or quartered if
large, cut into 2-inch chunks**

1 tablespoon butter

**1 tablespoon fresh tangerine, clementine,
or orange juice, plus more for serving**

**1 teaspoon fennel seeds, lightly crushed
in a mortar and pestle or with the side of
a heavy knife (optional)**

¼ teaspoon kosher salt

½ cup fresh ricotta

2 tablespoons chopped fresh chives

Extra-virgin olive oil, to taste

Flaky sea salt, to taste

Sweet carrots get even sweeter when caramelized in butter, then cooked until silky soft in the pressure cooker. The better your ricotta, the better this very simple dish will turn out—for the most deluxe dish, consider making your own (see page 21). Or skip the ricotta and top the carrots with crumbled feta, goat cheese, or even cubed fresh mozzarella. Anything creamy will work nicely. And if you don't like walnuts, substitute any kind of nut you do like. This dish really benefits from the crunch.

---

1. Heat the oven to 350°F.

2. Spread the nuts on a small rimmed baking sheet and bake until lightly browned, about 10 minutes. Once they have cooled, give them a rough chop.

3. In the pressure cooker, combine the carrots, butter, tangerine juice, fennel seeds, and salt. Cover and cook on high pressure for 2 to 3 minutes, depending on how soft you like your carrots. Release the pressure manually. Turn the sauté function on, and cook until the carrots start to caramelize, occasionally tossing them gently for even browning.

4. Transfer the carrots to a serving platter, and toss them with another squeeze of tangerine juice. Dollop with the ricotta, and then top with the chives, walnuts, a drizzle of olive oil, and sea salt to taste.

ARTICHOKES
WITH GARLIC MAYONNAISE

TIME: 30 MINUTES

YIELD: 4 SERVINGS

GF · P · VEG

———

2 to 3 garlic cloves

4 medium artichokes

½ lemon, plus 1 teaspoon lemon juice, or more to taste

Kosher salt, to taste

⅛ teaspoon fine sea salt, plus more to taste

1 large egg

1 large egg yolk

¾ cup extra-virgin olive oil

———

The electric pressure cooker is wonderful for artichokes, making them weeknight-accessible since they cook so quickly. The garlic mayonnaise is a rich and creamy touch, but you can certainly skip it and serve these with a bowl of melted butter or olive oil for dipping instead. Or serve them on their own with a squeeze of lemon. If you love artichokes, you don't need anything added to enjoy them.

———

1. Pour 1 cup of water into the pressure cooker. Smash 1 garlic clove and add it to the water.

2. To prepare the artichokes, cut off the stems and rub the stems' cut ends with the lemon half to prevent discoloration. Peel off the tough outer layer of the stems with a vegetable peeler, and then rub the stems with the lemon, too. Place the stems in the water, and set the steamer basket on top of the stems.

3. Cut off the top third of each artichoke, and rub the cut ends with the lemon. Pull off the outer layer of tough leaves (10 to 15 leaves) of each artichoke. Rub the artichokes all over with the lemon half, and place them facing up in the steamer basket. Sprinkle with a little kosher salt, cover, and cook on high pressure for 10 minutes. Release the pressure manually. (Cook for 5 minutes if using small artichokes, and 15 minutes if using large ones.)

4. Meanwhile, make the garlic mayonnaise: Grate the remaining garlic clove (or use 2 cloves if you like it very garlicky) into a blender, and then add the lemon juice and sea salt. Let it sit for 1 minute. Then add the egg and egg yolk, and blend briefly to combine. With the blender running, pour in the oil in a steady stream until the aioli is thick and creamy. Taste, and add more salt, pepper, and/or lemon juice if necessary.

5. Serve the artichokes with the aioli on the side for dipping.

MASHED POTATOES
WITH SOUR CREAM + CHIVES

TIME: 20 MINUTES

YIELD: 6 TO 8 SERVINGS

GF · VEG

————

1 tablespoon plus 1 teaspoon kosher salt

3 pounds Yukon Gold potatoes, peeled and cut into 1-inch chunks

5 tablespoons unsalted butter, at room temperature

1 cup sour cream, at room temperature

¼ teaspoon freshly ground black pepper

3 tablespoons finely chopped fresh chives

⅓ cup freshly grated Parmesan cheese, or to taste

————

This recipe gives you everything you want in a dish of mashed potatoes: supreme creaminess from both butter and sour cream, a deep potato flavor, a little Parmesan for a salty tang, and chives for color and freshness. That said, if you want to bring the fat content down, you can use less butter (as little as 2 tablespoons will still work). But don't skimp on the sour cream, which is necessary for both flavor and texture.

————

1. Put 1 cup of warm water and the 1 tablespoon salt in the pressure cooker and stir until the salt dissolves. Insert the steamer basket and place the potatoes in the basket.

2. Cover, and cook on high pressure for 8 minutes. Release the pressure manually.

3. Transfer the potatoes to a bowl. Add the butter, sour cream, remaining 1 teaspoon salt, and the pepper and use a potato masher or fork to mash everything together. Add the chives and mix well. Adjust the seasoning to taste, if necessary. Sprinkle with the Parmesan cheese just before serving.

GREEN BEANS, ITALIAN GRANDMA-STYLE

TIME: 20 MINUTES

YIELD: 4 TO 6 SERVINGS

GF · V · VEG

---

2 tablespoons extra-virgin olive oil, plus more for serving

4 garlic cloves, smashed

2 tablespoons drained capers

¼ teaspoon kosher salt, plus more as needed

Large pinch of crushed red pepper flakes

1 pound fresh green beans, trimmed

½ cup diced fresh tomatoes

2 sprigs fresh rosemary

1 teaspoon red wine vinegar or balsamic vinegar (red wine is sharper; balsamic is sweeter), plus more if needed

Freshly cracked black pepper to taste

A pot full of tender green beans stewing with tomatoes, garlic, rosemary, and capers is the kind of thing you might see simmering on the stove in somebody's Italian grandmother's kitchen—it's both savory and deeply comforting. You can serve the beans as a side dish with any kind of meat, fish, or pasta, but I also love eating a big bowl of this on its own for dinner, maybe with some crusty bread on the side to mop up all the glorious, garlicky sauce. Anchovy lovers, feel free to add a few fillets to the pot. Note that these green beans are of the soft and very tender variety—they do lose their crunch in the pressure cooker. And that is the delectable point here.

---

1. Using the sauté function, heat the oil in the pressure cooker until it is hot. Add the garlic and sauté until it turns golden brown around the edges, 1 to 2 minutes. Add the capers, salt, and the red pepper flakes, and sauté for another few seconds.

2. Add the beans, tomatoes, and rosemary sprigs to the pot. Cover, and cook on high pressure for 2 minutes for crisp beans or 3 minutes for fully cooked beans. Release the pressure manually. Discard the rosemary sprigs. Stir in the vinegar, black pepper, and more salt to taste. Serve drizzled with more olive oil if you like.

BUTTER-BRAISED YUKON GOLD POTATOES

TIME: 15 MINUTES

YIELD: 4 SERVINGS

GF • VEG (USING HOMEMADE
VEGETABLE BROTH, PAGE 115)

———

**6 medium Yukon Gold potatoes
(about 2 pounds)**

1 to 2 tablespoons unsalted butter

**⅓ cup stock of choice
(chicken, vegetable, meat),
preferably homemade (see page 114)**

Large pinch of salt, plus more to taste

Freshly ground black pepper to taste

**2 scallions (white and light green
parts), thinly sliced, or 2 tablespoons
minced chives**

———

Tender and velvety, these potatoes absorb the butter and stock as they cook, becoming rich and extremely flavorful. Make sure to use good stock here, preferably from a batch you've made in your pressure cooker, or at least your favorite store-bought brand. After all, if the stock doesn't taste good on its own, it's not going to do your potatoes any favors. Don't overlook the scallions or chives at the end—they add a lot in terms of oniony freshness. Scallions will be the more pungent and crunchier choice; chives are milder and softer. Or substitute other herbs. Basil, tarragon, or mint will all add the necessary zing.

———

1. Peel the potatoes if you like, and slice them into ½-inch-thick rounds.

2. Place the potatoes in the pressure cooker and add the butter, stock, and salt. Cover and cook on low pressure for 8 minutes. Release the pressure manually.

3. Taste, and add the pepper along with more salt if needed. Stir in the scallions and serve.

MAPLE CHILE-GLAZED SWEET POTATOES

TIME: 20 MINUTES

YIELD: 3 OR 4 SERVINGS

GF • VEG

4 tablespoons (½ stick) butter

2 tablespoons pure maple syrup

2 tablespoons fresh orange juice or apple cider

½ teaspoon kosher salt

½ teaspoon ancho or New Mexico chile powder, or to taste

2 large sweet potatoes, peeled and cut into ½-inch-thick slices

Glossy, syrupy, and velvet-soft, these are like candied yams, but with a bite from the chile powder. Adding a splash of either orange juice or apple cider gives the potatoes a mild fruit flavor, with orange juice being the tangier, brighter option while the cider is sweeter and more autumnal.

1. Using the sauté function, melt the butter in the pressure cooker. Stir in the maple syrup, orange juice, salt, and chili powder. Add the potatoes and toss to coat. Then cover and cook on high pressure for 3 minutes. Release the pressure manually.

2. Transfer the potatoes to a platter, spoon the maple-chile sauce over them, and serve.

BUTTERNUT SQUASH
WITH TAHINI, POMEGRANATE + MINT

TIME: 25 MINUTES

YIELD: 4 TO 6 SERVINGS

V · VEG

———

1 medium butternut squash (about 2½ pounds)

Kosher salt, as needed

¼ cup tahini

1 small garlic clove, grated on a Microplane or minced

1½ teaspoons fresh lemon juice

Freshly ground black pepper to taste

2 to 3 tablespoons ice water

Extra-virgin olive oil, as needed

Pomegranate molasses or balsamic vinegar, for serving

Pomegranate seeds, for serving (optional)

Torn fresh mint leaves (or basil), for serving

———

In this Middle Eastern–inspired dish, creamy tahini sauce, spiked with a little lemon and garlic, adds richness and pungency to sweet butternut squash. As for peeling the squash, you can use a knife, but I think a vegetable peeler is the fastest and easiest way to get the job done. Or leave the skin on; it's completely edible and adds some texture to the mix. If you don't have any pomegranate molasses, substitute balsamic vinegar.

———

1. Peel the butternut squash if you like; then halve it lengthwise. Scoop out the seeds. Cut each piece in half lengthwise, so you end up with 4 long quarters.

2. Pour 1 cup of water into the pressure cooker pot and insert the steamer rack. Add the squash quarters, alternating the direction so that they fit snugly into the basket. Sprinkle with salt to taste; then cover and cook at high pressure for 6 minutes.

3. Meanwhile, in a small bowl, whisk together the tahini, garlic, lemon juice, and salt and pepper to taste. Then drizzle in enough ice water to make the sauce creamy (a couple of tablespoons or so).

4. Release the pressure manually. Use tongs or oven mitts to remove the steamer basket. Allow the squash to cool slightly in the steamer basket; then transfer it to a serving dish and drizzle with olive oil.

5. To serve, drizzle the tahini sauce and pomegranate molasses over the squash, and top with pomegranate seeds and mint leaves.

DESSERTS

BUTTERSCOTCH
WHITE
CHOCOLATE
PUDDING

**TIME: 1 HOUR,
PLUS AT LEAST 3 HOURS CHILLING
YIELD: 6 SERVINGS
VEG**

———

1½ cups heavy cream

½ cup whole milk

**6 ounces Dulcey blond chocolate
(caramelized white chocolate), chopped
(see note), or butterscotch chips**

5 large egg yolks

⅓ cup packed dark brown sugar

1 tablespoon vanilla extract

2 teaspoons dark rum, or to taste

½ teaspoon ground cardamom or nutmeg

⅛ teaspoon kosher salt

**Crème fraîche or whipped cream,
for serving**

**Chocolate shavings, for serving
(optional)**

———

If you adore butterscotch pudding, this extra-rich version, scented with spices and dark rum, is well worth the effort. It calls for an unusual ingredient: caramelized white chocolate. Valrhona makes a version called Dulcey. Or you can easily make your own using whatever kind of white chocolate you can find. It does add an extra step but it's not at all difficult to do. And if you're a huge caramel fan, I'd recommend caramelizing a couple extra ounces of white chocolate so you can nibble on it while your pudding cooks. As a last resort, you can also use butterscotch chips, though the flavor won't be nearly as nuanced.

———

1. In a heavy saucepan, bring the cream and milk to a simmer. Remove the pan from the heat, and whisk in the caramelized white chocolate until it is melted and smooth.

2. In a large bowl, whisk together the egg yolks, brown sugar, vanilla, rum, cardamom or nutmeg, and salt. Whisking constantly, pour the hot chocolate into the yolk mixture, whisking vigorously until the mixture is smooth. Strain it through a very fine mesh sieve into a large measuring cup or bowl. The pudding mixture can be made up to 2 days ahead and stored, covered, in the refrigerator.

3. Divide the chocolate mixture among six 4- to 6-ounce custard cups, espresso cups, or small ramekins and cover each cup with a piece of aluminum foil. Or pour the whole amount into a 1-quart soufflé dish, and cover it with foil.

4. Insert a steamer rack into the pressure cooker and fill with 1½ cups of water. You can cook the custards in two batches: Place 3 custard cups on the steamer rack, cover, and cook on low pressure for 4 minutes. Let the pressure release naturally for 5 minutes; then release the remaining pressure manually. Repeat with the second batch. (Alternatively, cook all 6 at once: Arrange 3 custard cups on the steamer rack, then 3 more on top of the first layer, staggering the second layer of cups so they sit on top of the first layer; or insert a second rack between them if possible.) Cook on low pressure for 5 minutes. Let the pressure release naturally for 5 minutes, and then release the remaining pressure manually. (Note that the puddings may not cook quite as evenly when stacked as when cooked in batches.)

Or, if you are cooking the pudding in a soufflé dish, lower the dish onto the rack in the pressure cooker, using a sling if necessary (see page 15). Cook on low pressure for 18 minutes. Let the pressure release naturally for 5 minutes, and then release the remaining pressure manually.

5. When the puddings are cooked, use oven mitts to remove them from the pressure cooker. Remove the foil covers to allow the steam to evaporate and let the puddings cool to room temperature. Then cover the puddings with plastic wrap and refrigerate them for at least 3 hours and up to 3 days.

6. To serve, top the puddings with crème fraîche and chocolate shavings if you like.

Note: Valrhona makes Dulcey, caramelized white chocolate pastilles, which you can order online. Or to make your own caramelized white chocolate: Heat the oven to 250°F. Spread 6 or more ounces of cubed white chocolate on a rimmed baking sheet, and bake until the chocolate is the color of dark peanut butter, stirring every 10 minutes, 30 to 60 minutes total.

BITTERSWEET CHOCOLATE PUDDING

**TIME: 1 HOUR,
PLUS AT LEAST 3 HOURS CHILLING
YIELD: 6 SERVINGS
GF · VEG**

1½ cups heavy cream

½ cup whole milk

**6 ounces bittersweet chocolate
(preferably between 60% and 65% cacao),
chopped**

4 large egg yolks

1 large egg

⅓ cup sugar

1 teaspoon vanilla extract

⅛ teaspoon kosher salt

Whipped cream, for serving (optional)

Whether you call them puddings or *pots de crème* as the French do, these velvety bittersweet chocolate custards are creamy and rich. I like to make them in individual ramekins, which is a convenient and elegant way to serve them and also a subtle way of exercising portion control. Faced with the pudding in one large soufflé dish, I wouldn't know where to stop, and this chocolate confection makes it nearly impossible to put the spoon down. That said, if you'd prefer to cook it in a 7-inch soufflé dish, you can.

---

1. In a heavy saucepan, bring the cream and milk to a simmer. Remove the pan from the heat, and whisk in the chocolate until it is melted and smooth.

2. In a large bowl, whisk the yolks, whole egg, sugar, vanilla, and salt. Whisking constantly, pour the hot chocolate into the eggs. Strain through a fine mesh sieve into a large measuring cup or bowl. The pudding mixture can be made up to 2 days ahead, covered, and chilled.

3. Divide the pudding mixture among six 4- to 6-ounce custard cups, espresso cups, or small ramekins and cover each with a piece of aluminum foil. Or pour the whole amount into a 1-quart soufflé dish, and cover with foil.

4. Insert a steamer rack into the pressure cooker and fill the cooker with 1½ cups of water (see step 4 on page 144).

Or, if you are cooking in a soufflé dish, lower the dish onto the rack in the pressure cooker, using a sling if necessary (see page 15). Cook on low pressure for 18 minutes. Let the pressure release naturally for 5 minutes, and then release the remaining pressure manually.

5. When the puddings are cooked, use oven mitts to remove them from the pressure cooker. Remove the foil covers to allow the steam to evaporate, and cool the puddings to room temperature. Then cover the puddings with plastic wrap and refrigerate them for at least 6 hours and up to 3 days.

6. To serve, top the puddings with whipped cream if you like.

BREAD PUDDING

WITH DRIED CHERRIES + KIRSCH CRÈME ANGLAISE

TIME: 1 HOUR
YIELD: 6 SERVINGS
VEG

———

FOR THE PUDDING

Butter, for greasing the dish

4 large eggs

2 cups whole milk

½ cup sugar

2 teaspoons vanilla extract

Pinch of salt

3 cups dry white bread cubes
(such as baguette), in 1-inch pieces

⅓ cup dried cherries

FOR THE KIRSCH CRÈME ANGLAISE

½ cup heavy cream

½ cup whole milk

2 large egg yolks

3 tablespoons sugar

½ teaspoon vanilla extract

2 tablespoons Kirsch or brandy

COOK IT SLOW

———

Cook on high for 2 to 3 hours or
on low for 4 to 5 hours.

This custardy, not-too-sweet bread pudding is easy to adapt. If you don't want to use cherries, chopped dried apricots, mango, cranberries, or raisins will work nicely instead. You can also add ¼ cup chopped nuts if you'd like a bit of crunch, and/or ½ teaspoon cinnamon, ginger, nutmeg, or cardamom for a spicy note.

As for the sauce, while a custard sauce (such as the crème anglaise here) is traditional; dulce de leche (see page 155) is also a great topping, especially if you heat it up so it's runny before pouring it over the pudding. And no one would ever say no to fudge sauce.

———

1. Butter a 1½-quart soufflé dish. In a bowl, whisk together the eggs, milk, sugar, vanilla, and salt. Scatter the bread cubes and cherries evenly in the prepared soufflé dish. Pour the egg mixture over the bread and cherries, and cover the dish with aluminum foil.

2. Fill the pressure cooker with 1 cup of water. You can either insert a steamer rack into the pot and then lower the soufflé dish onto the rack using a homemade sling (see page 15), or, if you have a rack with an attached handle, lower the rack and dish together. Cover and cook on low pressure for 25 minutes. Allow the pressure to release naturally.

3. Meanwhile, make the crème anglaise: Combine the cream and milk in a medium saucepan and bring to a low simmer over medium heat.

4. Meanwhile, in a medium bowl, whisk together the egg yolks and sugar. Whisking constantly, pour the hot milk mixture into the yolk mixture; then return the yolk and milk mixture to the pan. Stir constantly over medium heat until it has thickened and coats the back of a spoon, 5 to 8 minutes. Remove the pan from the heat and strain the mixture through a fine-mesh sieve into a medium bowl. Stir in the vanilla and Kirsch. Serve the crème anglaise warm, or cover and chill it until needed (up to 5 days).

5. Using oven mitts, lift the soufflé dish out of the pressure cooker pot and place it on a trivet. Remove the foil. Let it cool for 15 minutes. Then serve it warm, or cover and chill it for up to 24 hours. Serve with the crème anglaise.

RICE PUDDING
WITH CARDAMOM
+ ROSE WATER

TIME: 1 HOUR,
PLUS AT LEAST 4 HOURS CHILLING
YIELD: 6 SERVINGS
GF • VEG

————

½ cup basmati rice, rinsed very well
under cold running water
until the water runs clear

3 cups plus 3 tablespoons whole milk

½ cup heavy cream

¼ cup sugar

8 cardamom pods, smashed
with the flat side of a heavy knife

Pinch of fine sea salt

⅓ cup sweetened condensed milk,
or to taste

2 to 3 tablespoons cornstarch

½ cup golden raisins (optional)

1 teaspoon rose water, or to taste

Ground cinnamon, for serving (optional)

————

This pudding has the satiny, wobbly texture of a classic diner pudding, but it is flavored with fragrant cardamom and rose water. For a more traditionally diner-esque flavor, substitute ½ teaspoon grated lemon zest or nutmeg for the cardamom, and vanilla extract for the rose water. And for a milkier, runnier texture, you can leave out the cornstarch entirely, though do still simmer the pudding at the end to thicken it a bit.

————

1. Put the rice in a bowl and cover it with cold water. Let it sit for 30 minutes to 1 hour; then drain the rice well.

2. Put the rice in a mini or regular food processor, or a blender, and process until it is coarsely ground. Put the ground rice in the pressure cooker pot and add the 3 cups milk along with the cream, sugar, cardamom pods, and salt. Cover, and cook on high pressure for 10 minutes. Let the pressure release naturally.

3. Once all the pressure is released, switch to the sauté function and add the sweetened condensed milk to the pressure cooker. Bring the mixture to a simmer.

4. In a small bowl, whisk together the cornstarch and remaining 3 tablespoons milk until very smooth. Add this to the rice mixture and let it simmer vigorously, stirring frequently, until the pudding thickens to taste, 2 to 4 minutes (remember that it will thicken up a lot more as it cools). Or you can skip this step for a thinner pudding.

5. Stir in the raisins, if using, and the rose water, and let the pudding cool. The slower the pudding cools, the thicker it will get. So depending on what kind of texture you'd like, you can either immediately transfer the cooking pot to a bowl of ice water to cool it quickly (a looser pudding) or let it cool slowly in the pot (a thicker pudding). Once it is cool, transfer it to a covered container and refrigerate it for at least 4 hours.

6. Before serving, sprinkle the top with cinnamon if you like.

FRESH MINT
CRÈME
BRÛLÉE

**TIME: 1 HOUR 45 MINUTES,
PLUS AT LEAST 4 HOURS CHILLING
YIELD: 6 SERVINGS
GF • VEG**

1½ cups heavy cream

½ cup whole milk

**1 small bunch fresh mint
(stems and leaves), about 1½ cups**

**1 vanilla bean, split, seeds scraped
out and reserved, or 1½ teaspoons
vanilla extract**

¼ teaspoon fine sea salt

4 large egg yolks

⅓ cup sugar

**2 teaspoons dark rum or peppermint
schnapps (optional)**

6 teaspoons turbinado or Demerara sugar

Steeping fresh mint in the custard of a crème brûlée gives it a fresh, bright taste that's different and somehow lighter-seeming than the usual recipe. However, if you'd prefer something more traditional, skip the mint and double up on the vanilla.

---

1. Combine the cream, milk, mint, vanilla bean and seeds, and salt in a medium saucepan and bring to a simmer over medium heat. Remove the pan from the heat, cover it, and let the mixture sit for 20 minutes for the mint to infuse. Discard the mint and vanilla bean.

2. In a medium bowl, whisk together the egg yolks, sugar, and rum if using. Whisk the warm cream mixture into the yolk mixture, and then strain the liquid through a fine-mesh strainer into a large measuring cup, pressing down on the solids. Pour the strained custard into six 4- to 6-ounce ramekins, and cover each one with aluminum foil.

3. Insert a steamer rack into the pressure cooker and fill the cooker with 1½ cups water (see cooking instructions on page 144).

4. Heat the broiler, with a rack placed 3 to 4 inches from the heat source.

5. Sprinkle each custard with 1 teaspoon of the turbinado sugar and then run them under the broiler for 3 to 5 minutes, until the sugar has darkened and caramelized. Serve immediately.

CLASSIC VANILLA BEAN CHEESECAKE

TIME: 1 HOUR 15 MINUTES,
PLUS AT LEAST 8 HOURS CHILLING

YIELD: 6 SERVINGS

VEG

FOR THE CRUST

¾ cup (75 grams) graham cracker crumbs
(9 to 11 graham crackers)

3 tablespoons unsalted butter, melted

1 tablespoon dark brown sugar

Pinch of salt

FOR THE FILLING

16 ounces cream cheese, softened
(see headnote)

6 tablespoons sugar

⅓ cup crème fraîche or sour cream

1 vanilla bean, split in half lengthwise,
or 2 teaspoons vanilla extract

2 teaspoons brandy

Pinch of salt

2 large eggs

Cooking cheesecake in the pressure cooker is one of those game-changing experiences. Not only is it faster than using your oven, it's also easier since you don't have to bother with a water bath. And you'll end up with the silkiest cheesecake imaginable.

Make sure your cream cheese is very soft before beating it. Consider microwaving the cream cheese (out of its foil package) for 10 to 20 seconds. Soft cream cheese is essential for getting a lusciously smooth texture here.

---

1. Preheat the oven to 350°F. To make the crust, combine crumbs, butter, brown sugar, and salt in a small bowl. Pat into the bottom of a 6- or 7-inch springform pan, patting it all over the bottom and ½ to 1 inch up the sides. Bake until golden brown, 8 to 12 minutes. Transfer it to a rack to cool.

2. Make the filling: Using an electric mixer fitted with the paddle attachment, beat the cream cheese and sugar until the mixture is very smooth (this could take several minutes). Then add the crème fraîche, beating again until incorporated. Use a paring knife to scrape the seeds out of the vanilla bean so that they drop into the mixer bowl (save the pod for another purpose). Add the brandy and salt and beat again until smooth. Beat in the eggs, one at a time, scraping down the sides of the bowl between additions. Pour the filling into the prepared pan, and cover the top of the springform pan with aluminum foil.

3. Fill the pressure cooker with ½ inch of water. You can either place a steamer rack in the pot and then lower the cake pan onto the rack using a homemade sling (see page 15) or, if you have a rack with an attached handle, simply lower the rack and pan together. Cover and cook on high pressure for 32 minutes. Let the pressure release naturally for 8 minutes, and then release the remaining pressure manually. Lift the pan out of the pressure cooker and transfer it to a wire rack. Remove the foil. Only the outside of the cheesecake should be fully set; the inside will set further as it cools. Let the cheesecake cool to room temperature.

4. Chill the cheesecake for at least 8 hours and preferably overnight. Release the springform sides to serve.

COCONUT CHEESECAKE

TIME: 1 HOUR 15 MINUTES,
PLUS AT LEAST 8 HOURS CHILLING
YIELD: 6 SERVINGS
VEG

FOR THE CRUST

½ cup (about 50 grams) graham cracker crumbs (6 to 7 graham crackers)

¼ cup sweetened shredded coconut, toasted (see note)

3 tablespoons coconut butter or oil, melted

1 tablespoon coconut sugar or light brown sugar

Pinch of salt

FOR THE FILLING

12 ounces cream cheese, softened (see headnote)

6 tablespoons sugar

¾ cup unsweetened coconut cream, at room temperature

1 tablespoon coconut-flavored rum, such as Malibu, or 1 teaspoon coconut extract

Pinch of salt

2 large eggs

Shredded sweetened coconut, for topping

Note: To toast the coconut, place it in a small skillet, set it over medium heat, and toast, stirring, until it turns golden brown, 2 to 3 minutes. Transfer the coconut to a plate to let it cool before using.

This velvety cheesecake is made with toasted coconut in the crust plus a shaggy garnish of shredded coconut on the top. As with the classic cheesecake recipe, make sure your cream cheese is very soft before beating it. If your kitchen is cold, consider microwaving the cream cheese (removed from its foil package) for a few seconds. Cold cream cheese is much harder to beat until smooth.

---

1. Preheat the oven to 350°F.

2. To make the crust, combine the graham cracker crumbs, toasted coconut, coconut butter, coconut sugar, and salt in a small bowl. Pat the mixture into a 7-inch springform pan, patting it all over the bottom and ½ to 1 inch up the sides. Bake until the crust has set and is golden brown, 8 to 12 minutes. Transfer the pan to a rack to cool.

3. Make the filling: Using an electric mixer fitted with the paddle attachment, beat the cream cheese and sugar until the mixture is very smooth (this could take several minutes if your cream cheese is not soft). Then add the coconut cream, beating again until incorporated. Add the rum and salt, and beat on medium speed until all the ingredients are incorporated and smooth. On medium-low speed, beat in the eggs, one at a time, scraping down the sides of the bowl between additions. Pour the filling into the prepared shell and cover the top of the springform pan with aluminum foil.

4. Fill the pressure cooker with ½ inch of water. You can either place a steamer rack in the pot and then lower the cake pan onto the rack using a homemade sling (see page 15) or, if you have a rack with an attached handle, simply lower the rack and pan together. Cover and cook on high pressure for 32 minutes. Let the pressure release naturally for 8 minutes, and then release the remaining pressure manually. Lift the pan out of the pressure cooker and transfer it to a wire rack. Remove the foil. Note that the center of the cheesecake will still be wobbly; it will set further as it cools. Top the warm cheesecake with the shredded coconut and let it cool completely.

5. Cover the cooled cake with plastic wrap and transfer it to the refrigerator to chill for at least 8 hours and preferably overnight to firm up. When you are ready to serve it, release the springform sides and place the cheesecake on a platter.

DULCE DE LECHE

TIME: 1½ HOURS
YIELD: 1 14-OUNCE CAN
GF • VEG

---

1 14-ounce can sweetened condensed milk

1 teaspoon vanilla extract or brandy

Large pinch of fine sea salt

A pressure cooker gives you dulce de leche in a fraction of the time it takes in the oven or in a pot of boiling water on the stove. Use it as a sauce for ice cream or bread pudding (see page 148), as a filling for cookies and cakes . . . or do what I do and eat it directly from the fridge with a spoon when no one is looking. Dulce de leche will last for at least three weeks in the refrigerator.

1. Remove the paper label from the can of sweetened condensed milk and discard it. Open the can and discard the top. Cover the opening of the can tightly with a piece of aluminum foil.

2. Insert the steamer rack in the pressure cooker and put the can of condensed milk on the rack. Add enough water to reach halfway up the sides of the can. Cover and cook on high pressure for 40 minutes. Allow the pressure to release naturally.

3. Transfer the can of milk to a wire rack, uncover, and let cool for at least 20 minutes; then mix in the vanilla and salt. Serve warm or let it cool completely.

STEAMED LEMON PUDDING

TIME: 1 HOUR 30 MINUTES,
PLUS COOLING
YIELD: 4 TO 6 SERVINGS
VEG

———

¼ cup golden syrup or honey

1 tablespoon plus ⅓ cup fresh
lemon juice

3 large eggs, separated

⅛ teaspoon fine sea salt,
plus more as needed

¾ cup sugar

1½ tablespoons finely grated lemon zest

1 cup whole milk

¼ cup all-purpose flour

2 tablespoons semolina flour

Fresh berries or chopped fruit, for serving

———

This rather British-sounding dessert is a bit like a sticky toffee pudding, but with a sharp citrus tang. The semolina gives it a pleasingly nubby texture and the golden syrup, or honey, forms a syrupy sauce when you unmold it. Serve it with berries or other juicy fruit (pineapple, oranges, mango) to contrast with the richness.

———

1. Pour 2 cups of water into the pressure cooker and turn on the sauté function. While you are preparing the pudding mixture, bring the water to a simmer, then turn off the pressure cooker and cover to keep water warm.

2. In a small bowl, whisk the golden syrup with the 1 tablespoon lemon juice. Pour into a 1½-quart soufflé dish.

3. Using an electric mixer, beat the egg whites and salt in a medium bowl until medium peaks form.

4. In a large bowl, whisk together the sugar, egg yolks, and lemon zest. Whisk in half of the milk, then both flours, then the remaining milk and the ⅓ cup lemon juice. (The batter will be very runny.) Using a rubber spatula, fold the egg whites into the batter. Then pour the entire mixture into the soufflé dish and cover it with aluminum foil.

5. You can either insert a steamer rack into the pot (be careful not to burn yourself on the hot water already there), and then lower the dish onto the rack using a homemade sling (see page 15) or, if you have a rack with an attached handle, lower the rack and dish together. Cover with the lid with the steam valve open, and turn on the steam function, and steam for 20 minutes.

6. Turn off the steam function, adjust the valve to the pressure setting, and cook on high pressure for 45 minutes. Let the pressure release naturally.

7. Carefully lift the soufflé dish out of the pressure cooker using oven mitts, and place it on a wire rack. Remove the foil. Invert a plate over the soufflé dish and, with the oven mitts on, quickly flip them over together, letting the pudding fall onto the plate. Let it cool slightly before serving.

ACKNOWLEDGMENTS

I have so many people to thank for helping to make this book come together in what was practically an instant.

First I have to thank my editors at the *New York Times* Food section, Sam Sifton, Patrick Farrell, and Emily Weinstein, for giving me the assignment to explore the world of electric pressure cookers in the first place. That started my obsession and I'm so grateful. This book wouldn't exist without them.

Then, of course, there's my darling agent Janis Donnaud, who is always in my corner.

The magnificent team at Clarkson Potter: My editor, Doris Cooper, and her assistant, Danielle Daitch; book designer Marysarah Quinn; the marketing and publicity team of Kate Tyler, Erica Gelbard, and Kevin Sweeting; Linnea Knollmueller in production and Amy Boorstein in production editorial; and publisher Aaron Wehner.

Our fantastic photographer Christopher Testani. The food styling genius Eugene Jho and his assistant Pearl Jones. And Sarah Smart and her assistant Katja Greeff, who curated the gorgeous props.

And finally I couldn't have done this without my talented recipe testers, especially Jade Zimmerman, who might be as obsessed with her electric pressure cooker as I am with mine. And thanks to Adelaide Mueller, Daniel Bernstein, and Lily Starbuck.

INDEX

Note: Page references in *italics* indicate photographs.